Careers in Focus

POLITICS

SECOND EDITION

Ferguson's

An Infobase Learning Company

Careers in Focus: Politics

Ferguson's
An imprint of Infobase Learning
132 West 31st Street
New York NY 10001

Library of Congress Cataloging-in-Publication Data

Careers in focus. Politics. — 2nd ed.
     p. cm. — (Careers in focus)
   Includes index.
   ISBN-13: 978-0-8160-8035-9 (hardcover : alk. paper)
   ISBN-10: 0-8160-8035-6 (hardcover : alk. paper)   1. Political science—Vocational guidance—United States—Juvenile literature.   2. Occupations—United States—Juvenile literature.   I. Ferguson Publishing.   II. Title: Politics.
   JA88.U6C28 2010
   324.273'012—dc22

                                                         2010049903

Text design by David Strelecky
Composition by Newgen North America
Cover printed by Yurchak Printing, Landisville, Pa.
Book printed and bound by Yurchak Printing, Landisville, Pa.
Date printed: May 2011
Printed in the United States of America

10 9 8 7 6 5 4 3 2 1

Table of Contents

Introduction

Careers in Focus: Politics describes a variety of careers in the world of politics—in local, state, and federal government; at newspapers, magazines, and publishing companies; at colleges and universities; in courtrooms and law offices; and in embassies and consulates throughout the world. These careers are as diverse in nature as they are in their earnings and educational requirements. Earnings range from minimum wage for campaign workers to $200,000 or more for federal and state officials, fund-raisers, lawyers, and lobbyists. A few of these careers—such as campaign workers—require little formal education, but are excellent starting points for a career in the industry. However, the majority of jobs in politics (such as ambassadors, city managers, Foreign Service officers, and political reporters) require a minimum of a bachelor's degree. The careers of lawyer and judge require a law degree, and political science professors need a doctorate.

Employment with the federal government is expected to grow about as fast as the average for all industries through 2018, according to the U.S. Department of Labor (DOL). Job opportunities at the state and local levels are expected to grow more slowly than the average during this same time span.

Careers in politics are affected by the issues and trends in society. Current issues, such as public safety, terrorism, protecting the environment, immigration, population growth and suburban sprawl, transportation, and cultural diversity will continue to be priorities in coming years. The Internet and other communication technologies will continue to require special attention as the government attempts to pass laws concerning privacy issues, copyright protection, and federal involvement in TV and radio broadcasting. Health care, taxation, education, and human rights will always be near the top of political agendas.

Campaign reform has the potential to change the face of future elections. Free broadcast time for politicians may improve the way candidates reach voters. The Internet has already become a new source for political research, public opinion polling, campaigning, and rumors. Candidates, consultants, and campaign workers will continue to use the Internet as carefully as they have broadcast and print media. They will also increasingly use Internet-related technologies such as the social networking site Facebook and the microblogging site Twitter to share their ideas with voters. This will help voters to be better informed about issues at hand and bills up for consideration by their state and federal lawmakers.

The articles in *Careers in Focus: Politics* appear in Ferguson's *Encyclopedia of Careers and Vocational Guidance*, but they have been updated and revised with the latest information from the DOL, professional organizations, and other sources. The following paragraphs detail the career article sections and other features that appear in this book.

The **Quick Facts** section provides a brief summary of the career, including recommended school subjects, personal skills, work environment, minimum educational requirements, salary ranges, certification or licensing requirements, and employment outlook. This section also provides acronyms and identification numbers for the following government classification indexes: the Dictionary of Occupational Titles (DOT), the Guide for Occupational Exploration (GOE), the National Occupational Classification (NOC) Index, and the Occupational Information Network (O*NET)-Standard Occupational Classification System (SOC) index. The DOT, GOE, and O*NET-SOC indexes have been created by the U.S. government; the NOC index is Canada's career classification system. Readers can use the identification numbers listed in the Quick Facts section to access further information about a career. Print editions of the DOT (*Dictionary of Occupational Titles*. Indianapolis, Ind.: JIST Works, 1991) and GOE (*Guide for Occupational Exploration*. Indianapolis, Ind.: JIST Works, 2001) are available at libraries. Electronic versions of the DOT (http://www.oalj.dol.gov/libdot.htm), NOC (http://www5.hrsdc.gc.ca/NOC), and O*NET-SOC (http://online.onetcenter.org) are available on the Internet. When no DOT, GOE, NOC, or O*NET-SOC numbers are listed, this means that the U.S. Department of Labor or Human Resources and Skills Development Canada have not created a numerical designation for this career. In this instance, you will see the acronym "N/A," or not available.

The **Overview** section is a brief introductory description of the duties and responsibilities involved in this career. Oftentimes, a career may have a variety of job titles. When this is the case, alternative career titles are presented. Employment statistics are also provided, when available. The **History** section describes the history of the particular job as it relates to the overall development of its industry or field. **The Job** describes the primary and secondary duties of the job. **Requirements** discusses high school and postsecondary education and training requirements, any certification or licensing that is necessary, and other personal requirements for success in the job. **Exploring** offers suggestions on how to gain experience in or knowledge of the particular job before making a firm educational and financial commitment. The focus is on what can be done while still in high school (or in the early years of college) to gain a better understanding of the job. The **Employers** section gives an overview of typical places of employment for the job. **Starting Out** discusses the best ways to land that first job, be it through the college career services office, newspaper ads, Internet employment sites, or personal contact. The **Advancement** section describes what kind of career path to expect from the job and how to get there. **Earnings** lists salary ranges and describes the typical fringe benefits. The **Work Environment** section describes the typical surroundings and conditions of employment—whether indoors or outdoors, noisy or quiet, social or independent. Also discussed are typical hours worked, any seasonal fluctuations, and the stresses and strains of the job. The **Outlook** section summarizes the job in terms of the general economy and industry projections. For the most part, Outlook information is obtained from the U.S. Bureau of Labor Statistics and is supplemented by information gathered from professional associations. Job growth terms follow those used in the *Occupational Outlook Handbook*. Growth described as "much faster than the average" means an increase of 20 percent or more. Growth described as "faster than the average" means an increase of 14 to 19 percent. Growth described as "about as fast as the average" means an increase of 7 to 13 percent. Growth described as "more slowly than the average" means an increase of 3 to 6 percent. "Little or no change" means a decrease of 2 percent to an increase of 2 percent. "Decline" means a decrease of 3 percent or more. Each article ends with **For More Information**, which lists organizations that provide information on training, education, internships, scholarships, and job placement.

Careers in Focus: Politics also includes photos, informative sidebars, and interviews with professionals in the field.

The field of politics holds exciting career paths that can appeal to people with a wide variety of interests and backgrounds. Take time to read about the diversity of opportunities in the political realm, and be sure to contact the organizations listed for more information.

Ambassadors

QUICK FACTS

School Subjects
Foreign language
Government

Personal Skills
Communication/ideas
Leadership/management

Work Environment
Primarily indoors
Primarily multiple locations

Minimum Education Level
Bachelor's degree

Salary Range
$58,000 to $100,000 to
$125,000

Certification or Licensing
None available

Outlook
Little or no change

DOT
188

GOE
N/A

NOC
4168

O*NET-SOC
N/A

OVERVIEW

Ambassadors are employed by the U.S. Department of State to manage the operations of the U.S. embassies in other countries. An embassy is the headquarters of a U.S. diplomatic mission established in the capital city of a foreign country. The United States maintains diplomatic relations with more than 190 countries of the world and has an embassy in most foreign capitals. One ambassador heads each embassy. Charged with the responsibility of maintaining diplomatic relations, an ambassador represents the president in matters of foreign policy. Ambassadors help to promote peace, trade, and the exchange of information between the United States and foreign lands.

HISTORY

Even in the earliest years of the United States, diplomacy was recognized as an important element of a strong government. People such as Benjamin Franklin, John Adams, John Jay, and Francis Dana were chosen for their intelligence, strength of character, and powers of persuasion to enlist the support of foreign countries for American independence. Benjamin Franklin was so successful in his commission to France that the French put his picture on watches, jewelry, and even snuffboxes. And the women of France had their hair done to resemble the fur caps Franklin wore. However, not all diplomats enjoyed such stardom; Francis Dana spent a cold, unproductive two years in Russia, unable to speak the language, and incapable of convincing Catherine II to support American independence.

Established in 1789, the State Department was placed under the direction of Thomas Jefferson, the first U.S. secretary of state and the senior member of President Washington's cabinet. It was his responsibility to initiate foreign policy on behalf of the U.S. government, advise the president on matters related to foreign policy, and administer the foreign affairs of the United States with the help of employees both at home and abroad.

Before the invention of radio, telegraph, telephone, and e-mail, the ambassador was entrusted to make final, binding decisions on behalf of the United States. More immediate means of communication narrowed the distances between embassies and their home countries; though today's ambassadors represent the president and actively contribute to international relations, they are more restricted in their powers.

THE JOB

Iceland. New Zealand. Venezuela. Sweden. Jordan. Egypt. Ambassadors to these or one of more than 190 countries that host U.S. embassies in their capital cities coordinate the operations of hundreds of government officers. An embassy serves as the headquarters for Foreign Service officers (FSOs) and other personnel, all working together to maintain a positive, productive relationship between the host country and the United States. Though the work is important, the post of ambassador is sometimes largely ceremonial. The president offers an ambassadorship to someone who has a long, dignified history of political service or to a wealthy supporter of the president's political party. An ambassador will stay at a post for two to six years. Career ambassadors are those who are Foreign Service officers; noncareer ambassadors are those outside of the Foreign Service.

Ambassadors address many different concerns, such as security, trade, tourism, environmental protection, and health care. They are involved in establishing and maintaining international agreements, such as nuclear test bans and ozone layer protection. They help to promote peace and stability and open new markets. When negotiating treaties and introducing policies, they help the people of the host country understand the U.S. position, while also helping the United States understand the host country's position.

Ambassadors spend much of their time meeting with government officials and private citizens of the host country. Together they identify subjects of mutual interest, such as medical research and the

The U.S. ambassador to the United Nations (*standing left*) huddles with ambassadors from other nations before a vote in the United Nations Security Council. *(Richard Drew, AP Photo)*

development of new technologies. They meet with those involved in private industry in the country, including Americans doing business there. When a country is struggling due to natural disasters, epidemics of disease, and other problems, they may pursue aid from the United States.

Ambassadors' work is not limited to the city in which the embassy is located. They travel across the country to learn about the other cities and regions and to meet the cities' representatives. Among the people of the country, ambassadors promote a good attitude toward the United States, as well as travel, business, and educational opportunities. When important U.S. visitors such as the president, first lady, and secretary of state arrive in the country, the ambassador serves as host, introducing them to the country and its officials.

Of course, ambassadors for different countries must address very different issues, such as environmental concerns, the state of education and health care, political structure, the agriculture, and industry. For example, the United States has entered agreements with Hungary, Thailand, Botswana, and other countries to establish International Law Enforcement Academies in those nations. The academies, jointly financed, managed, and staffed by the cooperating nations, initially provide training to police and government officials.

REQUIREMENTS

High School
In order to pursue any work that involves foreign government, you need a well-rounded education. Talk to your school counselor about the classes that will be most helpful in preparing for college. Courses in American history, western civilization, government, and world history are important, as are classes in math and economics. English composition will help you develop writing and communication skills. Any foreign language course will give you a good foundation in language study—many ambassadors know more than two languages. Journalism courses will help you develop writing and editing skills and keep you informed about current events.

Postsecondary Training
Many ambassadors and FSOs hold master's degrees and doctorates in international relations, political science, or economics. Many also hold law degrees. As an undergraduate, you should take general-requirement courses in English literature, foreign language, composition, geography, and statistics, along with courses for your particular major. There are many undergraduate majors relevant to foreign service, including foreign language, economics, political science, journalism, education, business, and English. You may also want to consider programs designed specifically for foreign service and international relations. The Edmund A. Walsh School of Foreign Service (http://sfs.georgetown.edu) at Georgetown University has undergraduate and graduate programs designed to prepare students for careers in international affairs. Many luminaries have graduated from the school, including Bill Clinton in 1968; former Secretary of State Madeleine Albright has served as a member of the school's faculty. Career ambassador is the highest rank for senior officers of the Foreign Service, but you don't have to be an FSO to be an ambassador. If you do choose to pursue work as an officer, the Foreign Service offers internship opportunities to college students in their junior and senior years and to graduate students. About half of these unpaid internships are based in Washington, D.C., while the other half are at U.S. embassies and consulates overseas. Interns may write reports, assist with trade negotiations, work with budget projects, or process visas or passports. The Foreign Service also offers several fellowship programs, which provide funding to undergraduate

and graduate students preparing academically to enter the Foreign Service.

Other Requirements

Ambassadors are usually already successful in their careers before being nominated for an ambassadorship. They also have some connection to top officials in the U.S. government. To achieve such success and good connections, you must be very intelligent and knowledgeable about government and politics. You should be comfortable in a leadership role and extremely ambitious and motivated. Those who serve as ambassadors have often achieved success in a number of different areas and have held a variety of powerful positions. You should be flexible and adaptable to new cultures and traditions. You must be interested in the histories of foreign cultures and respectful of the practices of other nations. Good people skills are important for dealing diplomatically with officials from other countries. All ambassadors must be U.S. citizens.

EXPLORING

As a member of a foreign language club at your school, you may have the opportunity to visit other countries. If such programs do not exist at your school, check with your counselor or school librarian about discounted foreign travel packages available to student groups. Also ask them about student exchange programs if you are interested in spending several weeks in another country. You can also participate in People to People Student Ambassador Programs, which offer summer travel opportunities to students in grades five through 12. To learn about the expenses, destinations, and application process, visit http://www.peopletopeople.com. Visit the Department of State's Web site http://www.state.gov to read the biographies of ambassadors around the world and for links to individual embassy Web sites.

The American Foreign Service Association (AFSA), a professional association serving FSOs, publishes the *Foreign Service Journal* (http://www.afsa.org/fsj), which features articles by FSOs and academics that can give you insight into the Foreign Service.

EMPLOYERS

Ambassadors work for the U.S. Department of State. They represent the interests of the president through the secretary of state. Many ambassadors are FSOs who have worked up through the ranks of the Foreign Service.

STARTING OUT

Those who are appointed as ambassadors have already succeeded in their individual careers. While many ambassadors have worked in the Foreign Service in some capacity, many others have established themselves in other ways. They have worked as directors in other government agencies and as members of the U.S. Congress. They've served on the faculty of colleges and universities. They have directed philanthropic organizations and run large companies. Before getting an ambassadorship, ambassadors may have already had a great deal of experience with a particular country, possibly having served as deputy chief of mission (the second in command of an embassy). Or they may have been involved in negotiating international agreements or in establishing new markets for the country.

ADVANCEMENT

After being nominated for an ambassadorship by the president, nominees are then confirmed by the Senate. Positions with the Foreign Service are rotational, so the length of an ambassador's term varies. Most ambassadors only serve a few years with an embassy. After leaving a post, they may go on to serve as ambassador at a U.S. embassy in another country. Some career ambassadors spend several years moving from embassy to embassy. Many ambassadors have published books on foreign policy, international affairs, and world trade.

EARNINGS

Ambassadors earn salaries that range from $100,000 to $125,000, according to the State Department. Entry-level salaries for FSOs are about $58,000. FSOs receive health benefits, life insurance, and retirement benefits that include a pension plan.

WORK ENVIRONMENT

Ambassadors are highly respected. They may have the opportunity to live in comfortable quarters in glamorous cities; or they may live in a struggling nation that is wracked by poverty and political unrest. Regardless of the area of the world in which they work, ambassadors have the chance to learn about a culture from the inside. Working alongside a nation's government officials, they are exposed to the art, food, industry, politics, and language of another country, while meeting some of the country's most interesting and notable figures. They also have the opportunity to play host to visiting dignitaries from the United States.

Most embassy offices overseas are clean, pleasant, and well equipped, but ambassadors may occasionally travel into areas that present health hazards. Customs may differ considerably, medical care may be substandard or nonexistent, the climate may be extreme, or other hardships may exist. In some countries there is the danger of earthquakes, typhoons, or floods; in others, there is the danger of political upheaval or terrorist attacks.

Although embassy hours are normally the usual office hours of the host country, other tasks of the job may involve outside activities, such as attending or hosting dinners, lectures, public functions, and other necessary social engagements.

OUTLOOK

Little or no change is expected in the number of positions available to ambassadors in the next decade. The United States maintains diplomatic relations with more than 190 countries, which means that there are fewer than 200 ambassadorships available. In recent years, the U.S. international affairs budget has been significantly reduced. Part of an ambassador's job is analyzing budgets to determine where cutbacks can be made. Experts worry that further cuts will not only hurt international trade but will result in disharmony among nations. Despite these budget cuts, the number of responsibilities of ambassadors and Foreign Service officers has increased; drug trade, nuclear smuggling, and terrorism are some of the issues confronting embassies today. Those people interested in protecting diplomacy and the strength of the Foreign Service need to closely follow relevant legislation, as well as promote the importance of international affairs.

FOR MORE INFORMATION

This professional organization serving current and retired Foreign Service officers has an informative Web site and publishes additional career information. To read selected publications online (including Inside a U.S. Embassy*), or for additional information, contact*
American Foreign Service Association
2101 E Street, NW
Washington, DC 20037-2916
Tel: 800-704-2372
E-mail: afsa@afsa.org
http://www.afsa.org

The U.S. Department of State has a wealth of career information on its Web site, along with information about internships, the history of the Foreign Service, and current ambassadors and embassies. For more information, visit

U.S. Foreign Service
U.S. Department of State
2401 E Street, NW, Suite 518 H
Washington, DC 20522-0001
E-mail: Careers@state.gov
http://careers.state.gov/officer

Campaign Workers

QUICK FACTS

School Subjects
Business
Government

Personal Skills
Communication/ideas
Following instructions
Leadership/management

Work Environment
Indoors and outdoors
Primarily multiple locations

Minimum Education Level
High school diploma

Salary Range
$30,000 to $50,000 to
$95,000

Certification or Licensing
None available

Outlook
About as fast as the average

DOT
N/A

GOE
N/A

NOC
N/A

O*NET-SOC
N/A

OVERVIEW

Campaign workers help candidates for government offices get elected. By calling voters, sending out fliers, and advertising on TV, radio, and the Internet, they educate the public about a candidate's strengths and concerns. Candidates for mayor, governor, Congress, president, and other local, state, and federal offices must use campaign workers and managers to handle many of the details of an election, such as budgets and expenses, fund-raising, and press relations. Campaign workers are needed all across the country, in cities large and small, to assist with primaries and elections.

HISTORY

"Tippecanoe and Tyler Too"—you may have heard of this song, an old tune from way back in 1840. It's not a folk ditty, but rather part of the presidential campaign of William Henry Harrison (known as "Old Tippecanoe"). Harrison, whose running mate was John Tyler, portrayed himself as a good ol' boy, pictured on leaflets with a bottle of cider in front of a log cabin. The tune, and the image, caught on, and it expanded the methods of campaigning to include slogans, press promotions, and "whistle-stop" tours (speeches at the railroad stations all along the campaign trail). Along with these new campaign methods, politicians also bought votes when they could, which led to campaign restrictions being passed in 1890. Variations on these concerns remain today, as government officials push for campaign reform that would limit the methods and sources of campaign funding.

In the last three decades, the broadcast media has become even more important in political campaigns. Campaign workers in the coming years will have to possess a good understanding of the use of TV and radio in gathering voter support. Campaign managers are also just learning how to best use the Internet. Maintaining a Web page, using social networking sites such as Facebook, and using Twitter have proven a popular way of educating the public about a candidate. Campaign workers will be involved in devising new methods of communicating with voters and attracting more people to campaign Web sites.

THE JOB

If you've ever run for student council or for an office with an organization, you have already walked on the campaign trail. Maybe you have even volunteered at the campaign headquarters of a candidate for government office. If so, then you've seen that a good campaign requires much more than a good candidate—it must also have devoted volunteers and an organized manager. Colorful buttons with catchy slogans, brochures outlining the candidate's strengths, posters on walls, and signs in yards—all these things contribute to drawing the voter's attention to your candidate.

Campaign workers help develop campaign tactics, prepare speeches and press releases, and arrange for the candidate to shake hands, kiss babies, and generally connect with the public. Depending on the importance of the office their candidate is pursuing and whether it's on the local, state, or national level, the campaign is composed of workers taking on different responsibilities. Every campaign should have a manager who will organize the talents of all those working on a campaign: volunteers, media and political consultants, pollsters, and others. "The candidate hadn't put much of an organization into place," says Claudia Lindley about her experiences managing a congressional campaign. "I set up the office, arranged for a phone account, fax machine, computer. I hired a staff and developed a strategy for asking for money." She also worked with a volunteer coordinator and the media people who created the radio and TV spots.

Campaign managers oversee fund-raising efforts, budgets, and expenses. Together with political consultants, they determine the public's interests and needs by analyzing public opinion polls and demographics. Then they produce ads and Web pages and arrange for media coverage that will allow their candidate to speak to those

A campaign manager (*right*) provides polling results to his boss, Tennessee state senator Mae Beavers (*left*), on election night. *(Larry McCormack, The Tennessean/AP Photo)*

needs. Campaign managers also direct volunteers in putting together mailers, making phone calls, and distributing signs and fliers.

REQUIREMENTS

High School
During high school, you should take government, history, math, computer science, and business classes. English, speech, and foreign language classes will help you hone your oral and written communication skills.

Postsecondary Training
You can volunteer on a campaign, or even manage one, without any college education. Because the level of work consists of making calls and stuffing envelopes, you will not need much training outside of the specifics of how to use the campaign office machines. But to manage a large campaign, and to work as a campaign director for such organizations as the Democratic or Republican National Committees, you will need a college education. You should major in political science, journalism, economics, history, or some other

undergraduate program that includes course work in English composition, government, and math.

Other Requirements

Claudia Lindley emphasizes the importance of self-confidence and energy when working as a campaign manager. People skills are important in organizing a campaign and in reaching the public. "You should be extremely assertive," she says, "without being abrasive." You should also have some sense of the industry and issues of the region in which you're working. You'll need the ability to analyze situations and statistics and to reach decisions quickly.

EXPLORING

There are many ways to gain experience as a campaign worker. You might help one of your friends run for student council, or even run for office yourself. You might also consider volunteering at the campaign office of a candidate who is running for local, state, or national office. Good workers are always needed to answer phones, prepare mailings, update Web sites, or perform general clerical duties. You may consider joining the local youth chapters of the political party of your choice. Contact the Democratic or Republican National Committees or the offices of another political party for more information.

EMPLOYERS

From campaigns for the smallest local office to that of the president of the United States, workers are needed. However, once the campaign is over, campaign workers usually lose their jobs. Campaign workers find more steady employment working for political consulting firms or assisting pollsters and other political researchers. They might also find work organizing the fund-raising campaigns of nonprofit groups, colleges, and other organizations.

STARTING OUT

Volunteer for local political campaigns and advocate for public policy issues of interest to you. You can even participate in national elections by volunteering at your local Democratic, Republican, or Green Party headquarters. Claudia Lindley first became involved in campaigning when the state she lived in was considering putting a low-level radioactive waste compound near her farm. "I got very involved, very quickly," she says. "I got in touch with people around the country." The skills she developed in the process made her valuable to candidates needing campaign workers.

ADVANCEMENT

After a successful campaign, campaign workers may move on to manage other campaigns, or they may go to work on the staff of the official they helped get elected. They may become political consultants, contracting with candidates in a variety of different races across the country and around the world. They could also advance into a position with the Democratic or Republican National Committees or become political director for an organization or association.

EARNINGS

Campaign workers who answer phones, prepare mailings, and post fliers are generally unpaid. Managers, however, can make around $30,000 to $50,000 a year for their work, or much more when working on a large campaign. A manager overseeing a budget of millions of dollars is paid well, as are consultants. Political consultants can make well over $95,000 a year. These earnings are paid for by the candidate or by donations from campaign supporters. Unless they work full time for an organization, campaign workers usually do not receive benefits.

WORK ENVIRONMENT

The work can be very stressful and require long days and weekends during a campaign. A manager must be available to the candidate at all times. Campaign workers may work in an active, energetic office, sharing in the excitement of a candidate's pursuit of office. But they may also be discouraged by the apathy of the general public in regard to government and politics.

The work can be tedious and exhausting, but those dedicated to a campaign usually receive recognition from the candidate. "You can distinguish yourself easily by actually doing the grunt work," Claudia Lindley says. "There are a lot of groupies who don't offer much to a campaign."

OUTLOOK

There will always be a need for motivated and hardworking campaign workers to help politicians reach voters and get elected. Those with knowledge of technology and the use of new media to reach voters will have the best job prospects.

FOR MORE INFORMATION

For information about political parties, election results, and campaign efforts, contact the following organizations:

Democratic National Committee
430 South Capitol Street, SE
Washington, DC 20003-4024
Tel: 202-863-8043
http://www.democrats.org

Green Party of the United States
PO Box 57065
Washington, DC 20037-0065
Tel: 866-414-7336
E-mail: office@gp.org
http://www.gp.org

Republican National Committee
310 First Street, SE
Washington, DC 20003-1885
Tel: 202-863-8500
E-mail: info@gop.com
http://www.gop.com

The following Web site provides information about all U.S. political parties and includes links to their Web sites:

Ron Gunzburger's Politics1.com
http://www.politics1.com/parties.htm

City Managers

OVERVIEW

A *city manager* is an administrator who coordinates the day-to-day running of a local government. Usually an appointed position, the manager directs the administration of city or county government in accordance with the policies determined by the city council or other elected authority.

HISTORY

There have been all sorts of governments and political theories in our world's history, and much of the structure of U.S. government is based on the theories and practices of other nations. The council-manager form of government, however, is truly American in origin. With government reforms of the early 1900s came government managers. Before the reform, cities were run by city councils or boards of aldermen. Because of rigged elections and other corruption by aldermen, a mayoral form of government was brought into practice. The council-manager form of government also evolved. Though a mayor is elected and holds political power, the city manager is appointed by the council. When the elected officials develop policies, the city managers use their administrative and management skills to put these policies into action. Some Southern towns began to develop council-manager forms of government as early as 1908; Dayton, Ohio, became the first large city to put the council-manager form into place in 1913. According to the International City/County Management Association (ICMA), more than 3,500 municipalities (communities with 2,500 people or more) operate in the council-manager form today. More than 92 million people live in these communities.

THE JOB

Have more bus routes been added to provide transportation to a new shopping area? Has the small park near the lake been cleaned up so children can play safely there? Will a new performing arts center be built downtown? These are some of the kinds of questions a city manager faces on the job. Even the smallest community has hundreds of concerns, from quality day care options for its citizens to proper housing for the elderly, from maintaining strong law enforcement in the city to preserving the surrounding environment. Every day, local newspapers feature all the changes underway in their communities. The mayor introduces these developments, speaking to reporters and appearing on the TV news and at city meetings. But it is the city manager who works behind the scenes to put these changes into effect. A city manager uses managerial experience and skills to determine what programs are needed in the community, to design the programs, and to implement them. The council-manager form of government is somewhat like a smooth-running business—the executives make the decisions about a company, while the managers see that these decisions are put into practice efficiently and effectively.

A city has many different departments in place to collect and disburse taxes, enforce laws, maintain public health and a ready fire department, construct public works such as parks and other recreational facilities, and purchase supplies and equipment. The city manager prepares budgets of the costs of these services and submits estimates to the elected officials for approval. The manager is also responsible for providing reports of ongoing and completed work and projects to the representatives of the residents. The city manager keeps in touch with the community in order to understand what is most important to the people of the city. A city manager also needs to stay several steps ahead, in order to plan for growth, population expansion, and public services. To oversee planning for population growth, crime prevention, street repairs, law enforcement, and pollution and traffic management problems, the manager prepares proposals and recommends zoning regulations. The manager then presents these proposals at meetings of the elected authorities as well as at public meetings of citizens.

In addition to developing plans and budgets, city managers meet with private groups and individuals that represent special interests. Managers explain programs, policies, and projects. They may also seek to enlist the aid of citizen groups in a variety of projects that help the public as a whole. They work closely with urban planners to coordinate new and existing programs. In smaller cities that have no planning staff, this work may be done entirely by the manager. Additional staff may be provided for the city manager of a large city, including an assistant city manager, department head assistants, administrative assistants, and management analysts.

A city manager's staff has a variety of titles and responsibilities. Changes in administration are studied and recommended by management analysts. Administrative and staff work, such as compiling statistics and planning work procedures, is done by *administrative assistants*, also called *executive assistants*. *Department head assistants* may work in several areas, such as law enforcement, finance, or law, but they are generally responsible for just one area. *Assistant city managers* are responsible for specific projects, such as developing the annual budget, as well as organizing and coordinating programs. They may supervise city employees and perform other administrative tasks, such as answering correspondence, receiving visitors, preparing reports, and monitoring programs.

REQUIREMENTS

High School

Take courses in government and social studies to learn about the nature of cities and counties. Math and business courses are important because you will be working with budgets and statistics and preparing financial reports. English and composition courses, and speech and debate teams are also very important, as you'll need good communication skills for presenting your thoughts and ideas to policy makers, special interest groups, and the community. Computer science is an important tool in any administrative profession. Take journalism courses and report for your school newspaper to learn about research and conducting polls and surveys.

Postsecondary Training

You will need at least a bachelor's degree to work as a city manager. As an undergraduate, you will major in such programs as public administration, political science, sociology, or business. The ICMA notes that an increasing number of local governments are requiring job candidates for manager positions to have master's degrees in public administration, business, finance, or a related field. Programs resulting in a master's in public administration (MPA) are available all across the country; some schools offer dual degrees, allowing you to also pursue a master's of business administration or master's of social work along with the MPA. The National Association of Schools of Public Affairs and Administration (NASPAA) offers voluntary accreditation to schools with degree programs in public affairs and administration. The association has a membership of nearly 270 schools, of which 59 percent are accredited. The NASPAA provides a roster of accredited programs at its Web site, http://www.naspaa.org.

Course work in public administration programs covers topics such as finance, budgeting, municipal law, legal issues, personnel management, and the political aspects of urban problems. Degree requirements in some schools also include completion of an internship program in a city manager's office that may last from six months to a year, during which time the degree candidate observes local government operations and does research under the direct supervision of the city manager.

People planning to enter city management positions frequently must pass civil service examinations. This is one way to become eligible for appointments to local government. Other requirements will vary from place to place. Most positions require knowledge of computerized tax and utility billing, electronic traffic control, and applications of systems analysis to urban problems.

Other Requirements

"You have to have the will, desire, and strength to want to lead an organization," says Michael Roberto, former city manager of Clearwater, Florida. He emphasizes that, as manager, you're the person held primarily responsible for the administration of the city. You should have a thick skin: "You'll be yelled at a lot," he says. In addition to handling the complaints, you must be able to handle the stress of the job and the long and frequently unpredictable hours that are required. "But you're only limited by your dreams in what you can create," Roberto says.

You will need to be decisive, confident, and firm in making managerial decisions. You need to be skilled at solving problems, while flexible enough to consider the ideas of others. Managers must also have a knack for working with people, have the ability to negotiate and tactfully debate with coworkers and other officials, and be able to listen to the opinions and concerns of the people they represent.

EXPLORING

You can learn about public administration by becoming involved in student government or by serving as an officer for a school club, such as a business or Internet club. A summer job in a local government office can give you a lot of insight into the workings of a city. Work for the school newspaper and you'll learn about budgets, projects, and school administrators. An internship with a local newspaper or radio or TV station may give you the opportunity to interview the mayor, council members, and the city manager about city administration.

EMPLOYERS

Cities large and small have council-manager forms of government and require city managers for the administration of policies and programs. Counties and suburbs also have managers. The ICMA reports that 58 percent of U.S. cities with a population of 100,000 or more use a council-manager form of government. Those with a master's degree in public administration may find work as a city planner. Other employment possibilities include working as an administrator of a hospital or an association, or in private industry. Some professionals with this background work as instructors for undergraduate public administration programs at universities or community colleges.

STARTING OUT

In addition to college internships with local public administrators, you can apply to the ICMA internship programs. There is heavy competition for these internship positions because they often lead to full-time work. The ICMA also publishes a newsletter announcing job vacancies. Nearly all city managers begin as management assistants. As a new graduate, you'll work as a management analyst or administrative assistant to city managers for several years to gain experience in solving urban problems, coordinating public services, and applying management techniques. Or you may work in a specific department such as finance, public works, civil engineering, or planning. You will acquire supervisory skills and also work as an assistant city manager or department head assistant. After a few years of competent service, you may be hired to manage a community.

Other avenues of potential employment include listings in the job sections of newspapers and professional journals. There are also private firms that specialize in filling government job openings. Jobs are also listed at the Web sites of professional associations, such as the International City/County Management Association.

ADVANCEMENT

An assistant to a city manager is gradually given more responsibilities and assignments as he or she gains experience. At least five years of experience are generally necessary to compete for the position of city manager. City managers are often employed in small cities at first, and during their careers they may seek and obtain appointments in growing cities. Experienced managers may become heads of regional government councils; others may serve several small jurisdictions at one time. Those city managers with a master's degree in business management, political science, urban planning, or law stand the best chance for employment.

EARNINGS

City managers' earnings vary according to such factors as the size of the city, the city's geographical location, and the manager's education and experience. Chief executives, the category that includes city managers, earned median annual salaries of $160,720 in 2009, according to the U.S. Department of Labor (DOL). In general, salaries for city managers range from $71,000 to $166,400 or more annually.

Salaries are set by the city council, and good city managers are sometimes given higher than average pay as an incentive to keep them from seeking more lucrative opportunities. Benefits for city managers include paid vacations, health insurance, sick leave, and retirement plans. Cities may also pay travel and moving expenses and provide a city car or a car allowance.

WORK ENVIRONMENT

Typically, a city manager has an office and possibly a trained staff to assist him or her. But a city manager also spends many hours attending meetings. To provide information to citizens on current government operations or to advocate certain programs, the manager frequently appears at public meetings and other civic functions and often visits government departments and inspects work sites. A city manager often works overtime at night and on weekends reading and writing reports or finishing paperwork. The manager also needs to attend dinners and evening events and go out of town for conferences. Any extra days worked on weekends are usually compensated for in vacation time or additional pay. "The long hours," Michael Roberto says, "can be tough on your home life, tough on your family." A city manager can be called at any hour of the day or night in times of crisis. Managers must be prepared for sometimes stressful interaction with coworkers and constituents, as well as the acclaim that comes to them for completing a job successfully or solving a particularly complex problem. "You're scrutinized by the press," Roberto says, and he emphasizes that a manager shouldn't be too affected by the coverage, whether negative or positive.

OUTLOOK

Although city management is a growing profession, the field is still relatively small. The DOL predicts that employment at the local government level will increase by approximately 8 percent through 2018, which is at a rate about the average for all occupations. However, few new governments are likely to form and, therefore, there will be few new job openings. Applicants with only a bachelor's degree will have the most difficulty finding employment. Even an entry-level job often requires an advanced degree. Those willing to relocate to smaller cities at lower salaries should have better job opportunities.

City managers are finding that they are sharing more and more of their authority with many different groups, such as unions and special interest groups. "This dilutes the system," Michael Roberto says, "and makes it harder to manage."

The issues that affect a city are constantly changing. Future city managers will need to focus on clean air regulations, promoting diversity, providing affordable housing, creating new policing methods, and revitalizing old downtown areas.

FOR MORE INFORMATION

For information on internships and to read Local Government Management: It's the Career For You!, *visit the ICMA Web site.*
   International City/County Management Association (ICMA)
   777 North Capitol Street, NE, Suite 500
   Washington, DC 20002-4201
   Tel: 202-289-4262
   http://www.icma.org

For more information on finding a school, the MPA degree, and public affairs work, contact
   National Association of Schools of Public Affairs and
      Administration
   1029 Vermont Avenue, NW, Suite 1100
   Washington, DC 20005-3517
   Tel: 202-628-8965
   E-mail: naspaa@naspaa.org
   http://www.naspaa.org
   http://www.gopublicservice.org

For information on cities, contact
National League of Cities
1301 Pennsylvania Avenue, NW, Suite 550
Washington, DC 20004-1747
Tel: 202-626-3000
E-mail: info@nlc.org
http://www.nlc.org

INTERVIEW

Michael Burns has been the city manager of Indian Hill, Ohio, for 20 years. He spoke with the editors of Careers in Focus: Politics *about his career.*

Q. Can you please briefly describe your primary and secondary job duties?

A. My primary duties include managing all city departments; budget preparation and management; personnel administration; preparing agendas and reports for city council and the city planning commission; executing agreements and contracts on behalf of the city; representing the city on various boards, committees, and at community functions; and responding to and directing citizen concerns and questions. My secondary job duties include providing counsel to department heads regarding issues, programs, and activities; maintaining files and records; and serving on professional boards and committees.

Q. How does the career of the city manager differ from that of the mayor?

A. The city manager is the chief administrative office of the city. He or she oversees the day-to-day operations, supervises personnel, prepares the annual budget, and executes the policies that are enacted by the city council. The mayor serves as the president of council. He or she presides over council meetings and serves as the elected leader of the community. Our charter prohibits the mayor from performing any of the responsibilities set forth for the city manager. In our community, the mayor is elected and serves without pay. The city manager is a paid professional public administrator.

Q. What are the main issues affecting Indian Hill today?

A. Indian Hill is an exclusive residential community with very high household income levels and a reliance on a local income tax that is the main source of general fund revenues. The continuing economic downturn, which began to hit the city in late in 2008, has significantly impacted tax revenues over the past two years. The city has responded to this downturn by cutting the operating and capital budgets for last year and this year by a total of 14 percent each year and spending down cash reserves. The economic conditions have also affected the housing market. Approximately 8 percent of the homes in the city are currently on the market, and sales are languishing because interested buyers are unable to sell their current residences and buy a more expensive home in Indian Hill.

Q. Do you travel for your job?
A. My job as a city manager involves some limited travel. I regularly attend the annual International City/County Management Association (ICMA) conference and two Ohio City and County Management Association conferences for professional development training. On occasion, I will travel to observe a project in another community or to attend some special training opportunity that is not available at one of the annual conferences.

I have experienced two international tours in connection with my city management profession. I visited St. Petersburg and Moscow, Russia, and Kharkiv, Ukraine, in 1994 as part of an exchange program pairing local government officials in Kharkiv with their American counterparts. My exchange partner also visited Indian Hill and stayed in my home for a month in 1993.

My ICMA affiliation also enabled me to participate in a study tour of local governments in Ireland. I joined 12 other city and county managers on an eight-day tour in 2001, which was hosted by a contingent of Irish ICMA members.

Q. How did you train for this job?
A. My formal training for the position of city manager included a bachelor's degree in urban planning and design and a master's degree in public administration. Most city managers today have a master's degree, usually in public administration. There tends to be a more broad range of majors for undergraduate degrees, including such majors as political science, civil engineering, criminal justice, education, prelaw, finance, and other business-related programs.

A city manager's training does not end with a college degree. It is incumbent upon all professional city managers to stay current with new technologies, new statutes and laws, and what we refer to as best practices, or new, successful programs and techniques which other communities have used to become more effective or efficient in their provision of public services. ICMA also sponsors a credentialed manager program, which certifies the proficiency of managers and helps individuals maintain that proficiency through participation in professional training opportunities on an annual basis. I annually log approximately 40 hours of continuing education. During the summer of 2003, I also participated in an intensive two-week Senior Executive Institute at the University of Virginia.

Q. How/where did you get your first job in this field? What did you do?

A. My city management career path began a year after I received my undergraduate degree from the College of Design, Architecture, Art, and Planning at the University of Cincinnati. During the first year after graduation, I worked as a planner in a small private firm in the Cincinnati area and lived in a small suburban community. The community advertised an opening for a planning and development director position and I was selected from a competitive field of candidates. The city had a tuition reimbursement program for employees who wanted to further their education, so I decided to participate in the program and increase my knowledge of government administration by seeking a degree in public administration. The University of Cincinnati offered an alternative "In-Career" program, which was geared toward students who were already working in government, and I was able to earn the degree on a part-time basis in about three years. Several years after receiving my master's degree, I began looking for a more challenging position in city management. I accepted my first management job as a township administrator in a rapidly growing township in the Cincinnati area. After four years in that position, I was recruited for the position of Indian Hill city manager, accepted the job in 1989, and I have spent the rest of my career in the same position.

Q. What are the most important personal and professional qualities for city managers?

A. There are several personal and professional qualities that are important for all city managers to possess. First, it is very important for a city manager to maintain the highest ethical standards in the performance of his or her duties. This is important, not only because most state statutes and local laws dictate high ethical standards, but also because managers set the example for all city employees and elected officials to follow in the fair and honest treatment of citizens, business vendors, and other public customers who come into contact with the city. Second, it is important for a city manager to be a leader of the organization he or she manages. This involves being more than just the boss. A manager must be able to lead an organization through change, when change is necessary; and a manager must be willing to take a position on important community issues, even when elected and other appointed officials may not agree [on] the best course of action on an issue. Third, a manager must be able to keep cool under stress and always maintain a professional demeanor. Community issues can at times be highly charged with energy and emotion, and the manager must be able to recognize the emotions, but not get caught up in them to the detriment of the community. Fourth, a city manager must be willing to put in the necessary time that the position requires. City management is not a 9-to-5 job. There are evening meetings and commitments and getting to the office early is sometimes the only way that a manager can get work done before the office opens for business and the phone starts ringing. A city operates 24/7, and the manager sometimes has to respond to important problems and issues at any time, day or night. You have to have a high level of stamina and dedication. Finally, a manager must be an active listener in dealing with the public and city staff.

Q. What are some of the pros and cons of your job?
A. The pros associated with the job of a city manager are all related to helping others achieve important goals and objectives. There is a real sense of accomplishment when an important project is completed or a perplexing community issue is solved to the satisfaction of all parties. It is also very rewarding to spend your career working with others who are in public service. People generally enjoy providing assistance to others and, when you are dealing with the public every day, there are plenty of opportunities to help community groups and individuals solve problems, answer concerns, and enjoy community events, programs, and activities.

The cons associated with the job of a city manager can generally be tracked to dealing with conflicts. There will always be issues and problems that cannot be solved to the full satisfaction of all the parties. A manager must be able to facilitate a solution that is in the best interests of the citizens or employees, even though some interested parties may not agree with the solution.

Q. What advice would you offer students as they graduate and look for jobs in government?

A. Graduates looking for jobs in government should be realistic about their career paths and be willing to put a high level of energy into every job, from their starting position to a manager position. In order for a new graduate to grow into a successful city manager, he or she has to understand the dynamics of city government at all levels, not just from the top down. Be diligent in the performance of your assigned tasks; be patient with citizens, customers, and fellow employees; and always strive to do the "right thing," and you will enjoy advancing your career in public administration.

Congressional Aides

QUICK FACTS

School Subjects
Government
History

Personal Skills
Communication/ideas
Leadership/management

Work Environment
Primarily indoors
One location with some
travel

Minimum Education Level
Bachelor's degree

Salary Range
$20,800 to $60,000 to
$114,400+

Certification or Licensing
None available

Outlook
Little or no change

DOT
209

GOE
N/A

NOC
N/A

O*NET-SOC
N/A

OVERVIEW

Congressional aides staff the offices of the members of the United States Congress. Working for senators and representatives, they assist with a variety of congressional duties, from administrative details to extensive research on legislation. Members of Congress typically include among their staff an administrative assistant, legislative assistants, a press secretary, an office manager, a personal secretary, and a legislative correspondent. Aides are generally divided into two groups: personal staff and committee staff. An aide may work in an office in Washington, D.C., or in a local district or state office.

HISTORY

Ever since members of Congress first began to hire stenographers and receptionists to assist with office duties, the role of congressional aides has stirred controversy. In the early 1800s, Congressmen worried they would look incapable of handling the responsibilities of their own jobs if they relied too much on assistants. This concern still exists today. Some members of Congress complain that having too many aides distances the senators and representatives from constituents, legislation, and the general requirements of their work.

Even these critics, however, admit that aides are very important to the lawmaking process. Since the end of World War II, with improvements in communications and transportation, voters have been making greater demands on their elected officials. Also, issues and casework have become increasingly complex. The Legislative Reorganization Act of 1946 was passed to allow each House and

30

Senate standing committee to employ a campaign staff of four professional and six clerical workers. Another Reorganization Act, passed in 1970, increased the number of professional staff to six members. The number of staff members has continued to grow, causing Congress to allocate more funds to construct new housing and office space.

THE JOB

Congressional aides see the lawmaking process at work—sometimes right on the Senate floor where laws are made. They work at the sides of important lawmakers, briefing them on legislation. The members of Congress (senators and representatives) rely on aides to assist them with a number of their responsibilities. Many constituents (the voters who elected members to Congress) rely on aides to help them make their voices and opinions heard. Aides answer letters, e-mails, and phone calls, and they distribute information to keep Congress members and the people they represent updated on the issues of national and local concern.

John Newsome worked on the staff of Congresswoman Barbara Lee as both a press secretary and legislative aide. Congresswoman Lee serves as the representative of California's 9th district and has been behind many important actions since taking office in April 1998. Lee was involved in declaring an HIV crisis in the local African-American community, making Alameda County the first jurisdiction in the nation to issue such a declaration. She helped get a grant from the U.S. Department of Commerce for BAYTRADE, an organization that promotes the development of trade relations between Northern California and the African continent. She has also played a part in modifying and passing a bill authorizing a study of the barriers that women face in science, math, and technical fields. It is the job of the congressional aide to inform the public and the media of these actions and also to prepare Congresswoman Lee for press conferences and interviews. During his time at the office, Newsome did just that and also researched legislation. "I've been interested in politics all my life," Newsome says. "I wanted to work for someone with a real eye to grassroots advocacy." When Congress was in session, his days started at around 9:30 A.M. and lasted until 9:00 P.M. or even as late as 11:30 P.M.

In the office of a senator or representative, aides either serve on a personal or committee staff. Committee staffs are strictly concerned with work that involves the construction and passage of legislation, while personal staffs also deal with matters concerning the home state. Personal aides are generally loyal supporters of their members of Congress and their political philosophies. But this does not mean that aides never have differing views. In some cases, aides may be more familiar with an issue and the general opinions of the constituents concerning an issue than the member of Congress. An aide's opinion can have an impact on a Congress member's decision.

The most important aide to a Congress member is the *chief of staff,* or *administrative assistant.* Those who achieve this position have worked closely with a Congress member for some time and have gained his or her trust and respect. The Congress member relies on the chief of staff's or administrative assistant's opinion and understanding of politics, legislation, and individual bills when making decisions. These aides also oversee the work of the other congressional aides.

Office managers run the office. They attend to the management of office clerical staff, which includes hiring, staff scheduling, and other personnel matters. In addition to administrative assistant secretaries who provide clerical support to the chief of staff, a congressional staff also includes *personal secretaries.* They attend to the Congress member's administrative and clerical needs, which include daily scheduling, managing expense accounts, and handling personal correspondence. *Mailroom managers* devise plans for handling the enormous crush of mail that arrives in congressional offices each day. They maintain mass-mailing records and prepare reports on mail volume and contents.

The legislative staff in a congressional office assists the Congress member with research of bills and other legislative duties. The *legislative director* directs the legislative staff and helps the Congress member keep up-to-date on important bills. They make sure the Congress member can make informed decisions on issues. Assisting the director are *legislative assistants* and *legislative correspondents.* Legislative assistants are each responsible for the coverage of issues in which they have developed some expertise. They brief the member of Congress on the status of legislation for which they are responsible and prepare floor statements and amendments for them; they may also write speeches for the member. Legislative correspondents are responsible for researching and drafting responses to letters received in the Congress member's offices.

Press secretaries are the primary spokespersons for members of Congress in their dealings with the media and the public. They respond to daily inquiries from the press, plan media coverage, coordinate press conferences, prepare press releases, and review daily newspapers.

State and *district directors* are responsible for state or district office operations, helping the Congress member to maintain close interaction with constituents. They represent their Congress member in all areas of the state or district and keep the office in Washington, D.C., informed on issues important to the local voters. Directors also plan the Congress member's visits to the state, sometimes accompanying him or her on a state tour.

A congressional staff also includes *schedulers*, who handle all the Congress member's scheduling of appointments; *database managers*, who are responsible for managing computer databases; and *caseworkers*, who work directly with people having difficulties with the federal government in such areas as veterans' claims, social security, and tax returns.

REQUIREMENTS

High School

A careful understanding of the government and how it works is important to anyone working for a member of Congress. You should take courses in U.S. government, political science, civics, social studies, and history and get involved in school government and school committees. Attend formal meetings of various school clubs to learn about parliamentary procedure. Writing press releases and letters and researching current issues are important aspects of congressional work. Journalism classes and reporting for your school newspaper will help you develop these communication skills.

Postsecondary Training

A well-rounded college education is very important for this career. Many congressional aides, such as chiefs of staff and legislative directors, have graduate degrees or law degrees. Consider undergraduate programs in history, political science, journalism, or economics. Political science programs offer courses in government, political theory, international relations, sociology, and public speaking. Look for internship opportunities in local, state, and federal government, and in political campaigns. Journalism programs offer courses in news reporting, communications law, and editing. Contact the offices of your state's members of Congress to apply for internships.

Other Requirements

Congressional aides need good problem-solving skills. They must have leadership abilities as well as the ability to follow instructions. Communication skills are very important, including writing, speaking, and listening. Before working as press secretary, John Newsome held other writing-related jobs, which involved writing grants and writing for the media. "I'm a very detail-oriented writer," he says. "I love writing. But to get a story sold also requires networking and advocacy. You have to maintain good relationships with people."

Aides must have a good temperament to deal with the stress of preparing a congressperson for voting sessions, and patience when dealing with constituents who have serious concerns about political issues. As with any job in politics, diplomacy is important in helping a Congress member effectively serve a large constituency with widely varying views.

EXPLORING

An extremely valuable—but highly competitive—learning opportunity is to work as a *page*. Pages serve members of Congress, running messages across Capitol Hill and handling many other support tasks. The length of a page's service varies, but opportunities are available in the fall and spring school semesters and during the summer. Students who are at least 16 years old are eligible to apply. Contact your state's senator or representative for an application.

You can also gain some insight into the work of a congressional aide through local efforts: Volunteer for various school committees, take an active part in clubs, and become involved in school government. Campaigns for local elections rely a lot on volunteers, so find out about ways you can support your favorite candidate. Keep up with current events by reading newspapers and news magazines. With an understanding of current issues, you can take a stand and express your opinions to your local, state, and federal representatives. By contacting your Congress members' offices, you'll be talking to congressional aides and learning something about their responsibilities. An annual publication called the *Congressional Staff Directory* (http://library.cqpress.com/csd) contains the addresses, phone numbers, and biographical information for members of Congress and their aides. Check with your school or local library to see if a copy is available.

EMPLOYERS

Congressional aides are federal employees. There are 100 senators and 435 representatives who hire congressional aides. This number won't change without an amendment to the constitution or the addition of another state. For fair representation in the U.S. Congress, each state is allowed two senators; the number of representatives for each state is determined by the state's population. California has the most representatives (53). Most congressional aides work in Washington, D.C., on Capitol Hill. Some find work in the home-state offices of their members of Congress.

STARTING OUT

Assistants are needed at every level of government. While in college, make personal contacts by volunteering on political campaigns. But be prepared to volunteer your services for some time in order to advance into positions of responsibility for candidates and elected officials. John Newsome has been involved since high school in grassroots advocacy. Over the years, he's been involved in HIV activism and community service with mentally disabled youth. Experience with these issues helped him to get his job with Congresswoman Lee. You can also gain valuable experience working in the offices of your state capitol building. State legislators require aides to answer phones, send letters, and research new bills.

Become familiar with the *Congressional Staff Directory*, which is available at your library or online. Getting a job as a congressional aide can be a difficult task—you may need to regularly submit your resume to placement offices of the House and the Senate. An internship can be a great way to get a foot in the door. The Congressional Management Foundation publishes information on internships, as well as offers internships to college students.

ADVANCEMENT

Advancement in any of the congressional aide jobs is directly related to a congressional aide's ability, experience on Capitol Hill, and willingness to make personal sacrifices to complete work efficiently and on time. The highest office on congressional staffs is that of chief of staff. It is possible for anyone on staff to rise up through the ranks to fill this position. Obviously, everyone cannot reach the top position, but advancement to higher staff positions is available to those who show they have the ability to take on greater responsibility. Legislative directors and state and district directors are probably the most likely candidates for the job of chief of staff. Legislative assistants, state office managers, and district office managers are in the best position to move into their respective directors' jobs. The top secretarial position is that of personal secretary, and any of the other secretaries can aspire to that position or that of scheduler. Any of the administrative staff, such as the receptionist or the mail room manager, can work toward the office manager's position.

EARNINGS

Congressional aides' salaries vary a great deal from office to office. Aides working in Senate positions generally have higher salaries than those working in House positions. Earnings also vary by position. A chief of staff, for example, has a much higher salary than a staff assistant working in the same office. Experience also plays a role in aides' earnings, with the highest salaries going to staffers with the most experience. Additionally, aides' earnings vary by the location of the office in which they work, that is, Washington, D.C., or the official's home district.

The Congressional Management Foundation (CMF), a nonprofit organization in Washington, D.C., publishes periodic reports on congressional employment practices that include salary information. In 2001, the average Senate salary for all positions (including aides) was $45,847. In 2000 (the most recent data available), the average House salary for all positions was $42,314.

According to CMF's *1999 Senate Staff Employment Study* (the latest information available for this publication), the average annual salary earned by a Senate chief of staff was $116,573. Senate office managers averaged $57,330; systems administrators averaged $39,612; and staff assistants averaged $22,504. These averages are for positions in Washington, D.C. CMF's *2000 House Staff Employment Study* found that the average annual salary for a House chief of staff was $97,615. House office managers averaged $44,009; systems administrators averaged $30,205; and staff assistants averaged $23,849. Again, these averages are for positions in Washington, D.C. More information on these reports is available from the CMF at http://www.cmfweb.org.

SimplyHired.com reported that hourly wages for congressional aides in November 2010 ranged from $10 to $55, or annual earnings of approximately $20,800 to $114,400, with a median annual salary of $60,000.

WORK ENVIRONMENT

Oddly enough, while Congress makes laws to protect workers and to ensure civil rights among the general populace, it has, in many cases, exempted itself from those same laws. Members of Congress contend that they should not be regulated like firms in the private sector because of the political nature of their institution and the necessity of choosing staff on the basis of loyalty. They also feel that it would breach the principle of the separation of powers if the executive branch had the power to enforce labor regulations in Congress.

Congressional aides are often faced with long hours, cramped quarters, and constant pressure. But many people thrive on the fast pace and appreciate the opportunity to get to know federal legislation from the inside. "The opportunities to meet people are endless," John Newsome says. "And it's incredibly challenging work." Despite the high pressure and deadlines, Newsome liked being a member of a staff involved in making positive changes.

OUTLOOK

Members of Congress will continue to hire aides regularly; however, this is not a large employment field. The need for new workers will be steady but limited. Additionally, aides' positions are linked to the success of the congressman or congresswoman for whom they work. If their employer is voted out of office, aides also lose their jobs. And, despite the long hours and often low pay, these jobs are prestigious, making competition for them strong.

Few people make working as a congressional aide a lifelong career. Those with excellent educational backgrounds and who are comfortable using technology should have the best chances for jobs. The Internet is making it easier for constituents to express their views quickly and to access press releases, information about current legislation, and the positions of their representatives. Advocacy groups will expand their use of the Internet, gaining more support and encouraging voters to express their views via e-mail, Twitter, and social networking sites such as Facebook. In the future, aides will work with a constituency much more knowledgeable about current legislation. The Internet will also serve aides in their research of bills, their interaction with the media, and their gauging of public views.

FOR MORE INFORMATION

For more information about House and Senate employment studies and other publications such as Congressional Intern Handbook, *contact*

Congressional Management Foundation
513 Capitol Court, NE, Suite 300
Washington, DC 20002-7709
Tel: 202-546-0100
http://www.cmfweb.org

Visit the Web sites of the House and the Senate for extensive information about individual Congress members and legislation. To write to your Congress members, contact
Office of Congressperson (Name)
U.S. House of Representatives
Washington, DC 20515-0001
Tel: 202-224-3121
http://www.house.gov

Office of Senator (Name)
U.S. Senate
Washington, DC 20510-0001
Tel: 202-224-3121
http://www.senate.gov

For employment opportunities, mail your resume and a cover letter to
Senate Placement Office
SH-116, Hart Senate Office Building
Washington, DC 20510-0001
Tel: 202-224-9167
E-mail: placementofficeinfo@saa.senate.gov
http://www.senate.gov/employment

U.S. House of Representatives
Office of Human Resources
102 Ford House Office Building
Washington, DC 20515-0001
Tel: 202-226-4504
http://www.house.gov/cao-hr

Federal and State Officials

OVERVIEW

Federal and state officials hold positions in the legislative, executive, and judicial branches of government at the state and national levels. They include governors, judges, senators, representatives, and the president and vice president of the country. Government officials are responsible for preserving the government against external and domestic threats, supervising and resolving conflicts between private and public interest, regulating the economy, protecting political and social rights of the citizens, and providing goods and services. Officials may, among other things, pass laws, set up social service programs, and allocate the taxpayers' money on goods and services.

HISTORY

In ancient states, the scope of government was almost without limitation. As Aristotle put it, "What was not commanded by the government was forbidden." Government functions were challenged by Christianity during the Roman Empire, when the enforcement of religious sanctions became the focus of political authority. It was not until the 18th century that the modern concept of government as separate from the church came into being.

The Roman Republic had a great deal of influence on those who framed the U.S. Constitution. The supreme council of state in ancient Rome was called the "Senate." Even the name "Capitol Hill" is derived from "Capitoline Hill" of Rome. The Congress of

QUICK FACTS

School Subjects
English
Government
History

Personal Skills
Communication/ideas
Leadership/management

Work Environment
Primarily indoors
One location with some
  travel

Minimum Education Level
High school diploma

Salary Range
$14,830 to $81,150 to
  $400,000

Certification or Licensing
None available

Outlook
More slowly than the average

DOT
188

GOE
13.01.01

NOC
0011

O*NET-SOC
11-1031.00

Fun Facts About Senators

- Three senators have participated in the Olympic Games: Wendell Anderson (hockey, silver medal), Bill Bradley (basketball, gold medal), and Ben Nighthorse Campbell (judo, no medal).
- Seven senators have won the Congressional Medal of Honor.
- Five senators have won the Nobel Peace Prize, with President Barack Obama being the most recent recipient.
- 16 senators went on to serve as U.S. presidents.
- 15 senators served on the Supreme Court.
- 51 senators have also worked as physicians.
- Only 38 women and 20 ethnic minorities have ever served in the U.S. Senate.

Source: United States Senate

the United States was modeled after British Parliament and assumed the powers that London had held before American independence. Limiting the powers of the individual states, the U.S. Congress was empowered to levy taxes, engage in foreign diplomacy, and regulate Native American affairs.

THE JOB

Think about the last time you cast a vote, whether in a school, local, state, or federal election. How did you make your decision? Was it based on the personal qualities of the candidate? The political positions of the candidate? Certain issues of importance to you? Or do you always vote for the same political party? As voters, we choose carefully when electing a government official, taking many different things into consideration. Whether you are electing a new governor and lieutenant governor for the state, a president and vice president for the country, or senators and representatives for the state legislature or the U.S. Congress, you're choosing people to act on behalf of your interests. The decisions of state and federal lawmakers affect your daily life and your future. State and federal officials pass laws concerning the arts, education, taxes, employment, health care, and other areas, in efforts to change and improve communities and standards of living.

Besides the *president* and *vice president* of the United States, the executive branch of the national government consists of the president's Cabinet, including, among others, the secretaries of state, treasury, defense, interior, agriculture, homeland security, and health and human services. These officials are appointed by the president and approved by the Senate. The members of the Office of Management and Budget, the Council of Economic Advisers, and the National Security Council are also executive officers of the national government.

Nearly every state's governing body resembles that of the federal government. Just as the U.S. Congress is composed of the Senate and the House of Representatives, so does each state (with one exception, Nebraska) have a senate and a house. The executive branch of the U.S. government is headed by the president and vice president, while the states elect governors and lieutenant governors. The *governor* is the chief executive officer of a state. In all states, a large government administration handles a variety of functions related to agriculture, highway and motor vehicle supervision, public safety and corrections, regulation of intrastate business and industry, and some aspects of education, public health, and welfare. The governor's job is to manage this administration. Some states also have a *lieutenant governor*, who serves as the presiding officer of the state's senate. Other elected officials commonly include a secretary of state, state treasurer, state auditor, attorney general, and superintendent of public instruction.

State senators and *state representatives* are the legislators elected to represent the districts and regions of cities and counties within the state. The number of members of a state's legislature varies from state to state. In the U.S. Congress, there are 100 senators (as established by the Constitution—two senators from each state) and 435 representatives. The number of representatives each state is allowed to send to the U.S. Congress varies based on the state's population as determined by the national census. Based on results from Census 2000, California is the most populous state and sends the most representatives (53). The primary function of all legislators, on both the state and national levels, is to make laws. With a staff of aides, senators and representatives attempt to learn as much as they can about the bills being considered. They research legislation, prepare reports, meet with constituents and interest groups, speak to the press, and discuss and debate legislation on the floor of the House or Senate. Legislators also may be involved in selecting other members of the government, supervising the government administration, appropriating funds, impeaching executive and judicial officials, and determining election procedures, among other activities. A state

President Barack Obama gives a speech. *(Cherie Cullen, U.S. Department of Defense)*

legislator may be involved in examining such situations as the state's relationship to Native American tribes, the level of school violence, and welfare reform.

REQUIREMENTS

High School

Courses in government, civics, and history will give you an understanding of the structure of state and federal governments. English courses are important because you need good writing skills for communicating with constituents and other government officials. Math and accounting help you to develop the analytical skills needed for examining statistics and demographics. You should take science courses because you'll be making decisions concerning health, medicine, and technological advances. Journalism classes will help you learn about the print and broadcast media and the role they play in politics. Take public speaking courses, as communicating verbally is fundamental to a career as a public official.

Postsecondary Training

State and federal legislators come from all walks of life. Some hold master's degrees and doctorates, while others have only a high school education. Although a majority of government officials hold law degrees, others have undergraduate or graduate degrees in such areas as journalism, economics, political science, history, and English. Regardless of your major as an undergraduate, it is important to take classes in English literature, statistics, foreign language, Western civilization, and economics. Graduate studies can focus more on one area of study; some prospective government officials pursue master's degrees in public administration or international affairs. Consider participating in an internship program that will involve you with local and state officials. Contact the offices of your state legislators and of your state's members of Congress to apply for internships directly.

Other Requirements

Federal and state officials must have deep concern for their constituents. They should be good listeners and be able to relate to people from all walks of life and understand their concerns. This attention to the needs of communities should be of foremost importance to anyone pursuing a government office. Although historically some politicians have had questionable purposes in their campaigns for office, most successful politicians are devoted to making positive changes and improvements. Good people skills will help you make connections, get elected, and make things happen once in office. You should also enjoy public speaking, argument, debate, and opposition—you will get a lot of it as you attempt to get laws passed. A good temperament in such situations will earn you the respect of your colleagues. Strong character and a good background will help you to avoid the personal attacks that occasionally accompany government office.

EXPLORING

If you are 16 or older, you can gain experience in a legislature. The U.S. Congress and possibly your state legislature offer opportunities for young adults who have demonstrated a commitment to government study to work as *pages*. For Congress, pages run messages across Capitol Hill and have the opportunity to see senators and representatives debating and discussing bills. The length of a page's service can be for one summer or up to one year. Contact your state's senator or representative for an application.

You can also explore government careers by becoming involved with local elections. Many candidates for local and state offices welcome young people to assist with campaigns. You might be asked to make calls, post signs, or hand out information about the candidate. Not only will you get to see the politician at work, but you will also meet others with an interest in government.

Another great way to learn about government is to become involved in an issue of interest to you. Participate with a grassroots advocacy group or read about the bills up for vote in the state legislature and U.S. Congress. When you feel strongly about an issue and are well educated on the subject, contact the offices of state legislators and members of Congress to express your views. Visit the Web sites of the House and Senate and of your state legislature to read about bills, schedules, and the legislators. The National Conference of State Legislatures (NCSL) also hosts a Web site (http://www.ncsl .org) featuring legislative news and links to state legislatures.

EMPLOYERS

State legislators work for the state government, and many hold other jobs as well. Because of the part-time nature of some legislative offices, state legislators may hold part-time jobs or own their own businesses. Federal officials work full time for the Senate, the House, or the executive branch.

STARTING OUT

There is no direct career path for state and federal officials. Some enter into their positions after some success with political activism on the grassroots level or by working their way up from local government positions to state legislature and into federal office. For example, President Barack Obama was a community organizer in Chicago before being elected to the Illinois state legislature and the U.S. Senate. Additionally, many politicians get their start assisting someone else's campaign or advocating for an issue. Those who serve as U.S. Congress members have worked in the military, journalism, academics, business, and many other fields.

ADVANCEMENT

Initiative is one key to success in politics. Advancement can be rapid for someone who is a fast learner and is independently motivated, but a career in politics most often takes a long time to establish. Most state and federal officials start by pursuing training and work experience in their particular field, while getting involved in politics at the local level. Many people progress from local politics to state politics. It is not uncommon for a state legislator to eventually run for a seat in Congress. Appointees to the president's Cabinet and presidential and vice presidential candidates frequently have held positions in Congress.

EARNINGS

In general, salaries for government officials tend to be lower than what the official could make working in the private sector. In the case of state legislators, the pay can be very much lower.

The U.S. Department of Labor reports that government legislators earned median annual salaries of $18,810 in 2009. Salaries generally ranged from less than $14,830 to more than $81,150, although some officials earn nothing at all.

According to the NCSL, state legislators make from $10,000 (Mississippi) to $95,291 (California) a year. A few states, however, don't pay state legislators anything but an expense allowance. Salaries of state governors are typically much higher.

In 2010, U.S. senators and representatives earned $174,000, the vice president was paid $230,700, and the president earned $400,000.

Congressional leaders receive higher salaries than the other Congress members. For example, the Senate Majority and Minority leaders and the President Pro Tempore earned $193,400 in 2010. U.S. Congress members receive excellent insurance, vacation, and other benefits. Benefits for officials at the state and local levels vary greatly, but often include medical insurance and pension programs.

WORK ENVIRONMENT

Most government officials work in a typical office setting. Some may work a regular 40-hour week, while others will typically work long hours and weekends. One potential drawback to political life, particularly for the candidate running for office, is that there is no real off-duty time. One is continually under observation by the press and public, and the personal lives of candidates and officeholders are discussed frequently in the media.

Because these officials must be appointed or elected in order to keep their jobs, the ability to determine long-range job objectives is slim. There may be extended periods of unemployment, when living off of savings or working at other jobs may be necessary.

Frequent travel is involved in campaigning and in holding office, so some people with children may find the lifestyle demanding on their families.

OUTLOOK

Employment of federal and state officials will grow more slowly than the average through 2018. To attract more candidates to run for legislative offices, states may consider salary increases and better benefits for state senators and representatives. But changes in pay and benefits for federal officials are unlikely. An increase in the number of representatives is possible as the U.S. population grows, but would require additional office space and other costly expansions. For the most part, the structures of state and federal legislatures will remain unchanged, although the topic of limiting the number of terms that a representative is allowed to serve does often arise in election years.

The federal government has made efforts to shift costs to the states; if this continues, it could change the way state legislatures and executive officers operate with regard to public funding. Already, welfare reform has resulted in state governments looking for financial aid in handling welfare cases and job programs. Arts funding may also become the sole responsibility of the states as programs such as the National Endowment for the Arts lose support from Congress.

FOR MORE INFORMATION

For more information about House and Senate employment studies and other publications, such as the Congressional Intern Handbook, *contact*

Congressional Management Foundation
513 Capitol Court, NE, Suite 300
Washington, DC 20002-7709
Tel: 202-546-0100
http://www.cmfweb.org

To read a blog about government-related issues, visit
Council of State Governments
PO Box 11910
2760 Research Park Drive
Lexington, KY 40578-1910
Tel: 859-244-8000
http://www.csg.org

To read about state legislatures, policy issues, legislative news, and other related information, visit the conference's Web site.
National Conference of State Legislatures
444 North Capitol Street, NW, Suite 515
Washington, DC 20001-1543

Tel: 202-624-5400
http://www.ncsl.org

For information on state governors, contact
National Governors Association
Hall of the States
444 North Capitol Street, NW, Suite 267
Washington, DC 20001-1512
Tel: 202-624-5300
http://www.nga.org

Visit the Senate and House Web sites for extensive information about Congress, government history, current legislation, and links to state legislature sites. To inquire about internship opportunities with your Congress member, contact
Senate Placement Office
SH-116, Hart Senate Office Building
Washington DC 20510-0001
Tel: 202-224-9167
E-mail: placementofficeinfo@saa.senate.gov
http://www.senate.gov/employment

U.S. House of Representatives
Office of Human Resources
102 Ford House Office Building
Washington, DC 20515-0001
Tel: 202-226-4504
http://www.house.gov/cao-hr

Foreign Service Officers

OVERVIEW

Foreign Service officers represent the government and the people of the United States by conducting relations with foreign countries and international organizations. They promote and protect the United States' political, economic, and commercial interests in other countries. They observe and analyze conditions and developments in foreign countries and report to the State Department and other government agencies. Foreign Service officers guard the welfare of Americans abroad and help foreign nationals traveling to the United States. There are approximately 11,500 Foreign Service officers working in Washington, D.C, and in nearly 265 U.S. embassies and consulates around the world.

HISTORY

The Foreign Service is a branch of the U.S. Department of State, which plans and carries out U.S. foreign policy under the authority of the president. Established in 1789, the State Department was placed under the direction of Thomas Jefferson, the first U.S. secretary of state and the senior officer in President George Washington's cabinet. It was his responsibility to initiate foreign policy on behalf of the U.S. government, advise the president on matters related to foreign policy, and administer the foreign affairs of the United States with the help of employees both at home and abroad.

Books to Read

Carland, Maria Pinto, and Candace Faber. (eds.) *Careers in International Affairs.* 8th ed. Washington, D.C.: Georgetown University Press, 2008.

Dale, William N. *Living Diplomatically: A Life in the U.S. Foreign Service.* Lanham, Md.: Hamilton Books, 2008.

Dorman, Shawn. (ed.) *Inside a U.S. Embassy: How the Foreign Service Works for America.* 2d ed. Dulles, Va.: Potomac Books Inc., 2009.

Kopp, Harry W., and Charles A. Gillespie. *Career Diplomacy: Life and Work in the U.S. Foreign Service.* Washington, D.C.: Georgetown University Press, 2008.

Lawrence, Malcolm. *Something Will Come Along: Witty Memoirs of a Foreign Service Officer with Nine Children.* Raleigh, N.C.: Pentland Press, 2003.

Linderman, Patricia, Melissa Brayer Hess, and Marlene Monfiletto Nice. (eds.) *Realities of Foreign Service Life: Volume 2.* Bloomington, Ind.: iUniverse, 2007.

The Foreign Service wasn't actually established until 1924, when the Diplomatic and Consular Services were brought together as one organization. The Foreign Service was formed in anticipation of a trade war; security issues became the service's focus with World War II and remained so throughout the cold war. With the end of the cold war, issues such as trade protection and combating terrorism have come to the forefront of the service's concerns. Other foreign policy issues facing today's Foreign Service officers include the global struggle to eliminate diseases such as AIDS, efforts to protect the environment, and international law enforcement regarding drug trafficking and science and technology issues.

THE JOB

Foreign Service officers work in embassies and consulates throughout the world. Between foreign assignments, they may have duties in the Department of State in Washington, D.C., or they may be temporarily detailed to the Department of Defense, the Department of Commerce, or other government departments and agencies.

James Prosser spent 36 years with the Foreign Service. Though he is retired, he visits academic and civic organizations to lecture about the history of the Foreign Service. As an officer, Prosser worked in the telecommunications and computer fields as an operator, engineer, manager, and international negotiator. He speaks German, French, and Italian. Among his experiences: In the then Belgian Congo, he ran a communications center and shortwave radio station during the country's postcolonial struggle for independence, a time when many were losing their lives in the upheaval; in 1967, France expelled the North Atlantic Treaty Organization (NATO) headquarters and Prosser was placed in charge of moving the U.S. communications elements of NATO to Belgium, as well as designing the new communications facilities there. Prosser has served in Germany, Italy, Kenya, and other countries. "Being in charge of all U.S. government telecommunications facilities in Africa and the Indian Ocean was an especially gratifying challenge," Prosser says. He still visits Africa whenever possible.

Foreign Service officers specialize in one of five areas: management affairs, consular affairs, economic affairs, political affairs, and public diplomacy.

Management officers who work in embassies and consulates oversee and administer the day-to-day operations of their posts. Some handle financial matters such as planning budgets and controlling expenditures. Others work in general services: They purchase and look after government property and supplies, negotiate leases and contracts for office space and housing, and make arrangements for travel and shipping. Personnel officers deal with assignments, promotions, and personnel relations affecting both U.S. and local workers. This includes hiring local workers and arranging labor and management agreements. Management officers based in Washington do similar work and act as liaisons between the Department of State and their overseas colleagues.

Consular officers help and advise U.S. citizens abroad as well as foreigners wishing to enter the United States as visitors or residents. They provide medical, legal, personal, and travel assistance to U.S. citizens in cases of accidents or emergencies, such as helping those without money to return home, finding lost relatives, visiting and advising those in foreign jails, and distributing Social Security checks and other federal benefits to eligible people. They issue passports, register births and deaths and other information, serve as notaries public, and take testimony needed by courts in the United States. In addition, these officers issue visas to foreign nationals who want to enter the United States and decide which of them are eligible for citizenship. Consular officers located in the Bureau of Consular Affairs in Washington provide support and help for their fellow officers abroad.

Economic affairs may be handled by one officer at a small post or divided between two full-time officers at a large post. *Economic officers* study the structure of a country's economy and the way it functions to determine how the United States might be affected by trends, trade patterns, and methods of setting prices. Their analysis of the economic data, based on a thorough understanding of the international monetary system, is passed along to their counterparts in Washington. Economic officers in Washington write position papers for the State Department and the White House, suggesting U.S. policies to help improve economic conditions in foreign nations. Other economic officers concern themselves with building U.S. trade overseas. They carry out marketing and promotion campaigns to encourage foreign countries to do business with the United States. When they learn of potential trade and investment opportunities abroad, they inform U.S. companies that might be interested. They then help the firms find local agents and advise them about local business practices.

Political officers overseas convey the views and position of the United States to government officials of the countries where they are based. They also keep the United States informed about any political developments that may affect U.S. interests, and they may negotiate agreements between the two governments. Political officers are alert to local developments and reactions to U.S. policy. They maintain close contact with foreign officials and political and labor leaders and try to predict changes in local attitudes or leadership that might affect U.S. policies. They report their observations to Washington and interpret what is happening.

Political officers in Washington study and evaluate the information submitted by their counterparts abroad. They keep State Department and White House officials informed of developments overseas and of the possible effects on the United States. They suggest revisions in U.S. policy and see that their fellow officers abroad carry out approved changes.

Public diplomacy officers prepare and disseminate information designed to help other countries understand the United States and its policies. They distribute press releases and background articles and meet with members of the local press, radio, television, and film organizations to give them information about the United States. Public diplomacy officers engage in activities that promote an understanding and appreciation of American culture and traditions. These activities may involve educational and cultural exchanges between the countries, exhibits, lectures, performing arts events, libraries, book translations, English teaching programs, and youth groups. Public diplomacy officers deal with universities and cultural and intellectual leaders. Many officers work on both information and cultural programs.

REQUIREMENTS

High School

Those who work for the Foreign Service will need to call upon a great deal of general knowledge about the world and its history. Take courses such as social studies, history, American government, and English literature. English composition will help you develop writing and communication skills. Any foreign language course will give you a good foundation in language study—and good foreign language skills can help in getting a job with the Foreign Service and make you eligible for a higher starting salary. Take a journalism course that allows you to follow current events and world news, as well as develop your writing and editing skills. Accounting, math, business, and economics classes will give you a good background for dealing with foreign trade issues.

Postsecondary Training

Though the Foreign Service is open to any United States citizen between the ages of 21 and 59 who passes the written, oral, and physical examinations, you will need at least a bachelor's degree to be competitive and to have the knowledge necessary for completing the exam. Most Foreign Service officers have graduate degrees. Regardless of the level of education, candidates are expected to have a broad knowledge of foreign and domestic affairs and to be well informed about U.S. history, government, economics, culture, literature, and business administration. The fields of study most often chosen by those with a higher education include history, international relations, political science, economics, law, business administration, journalism, English literature, and foreign languages. The Edmund A. Walsh School of Foreign Service (http://sfs.georgetown .edu) at Georgetown University has undergraduate and graduate programs designed to prepare students for careers in international affairs. Many luminaries have graduated from the school, including Bill Clinton in 1968. Former Secretary of State Madeleine Albright served as a member of the school's faculty.

The Foreign Service has internship opportunities available to college students in their junior and senior years, and to graduate students. About half of these unpaid internships are based in Washington, D.C., while the other half are at U.S. embassies and consulates overseas. As an intern, you may write reports, assist with trade negotiations, or work with budget projects. You may be involved in visa or passport work. The Foreign Service also offers several fellowship programs, which provide funding to undergraduate and graduate students preparing academically to enter the Foreign Service.

Other Requirements

As you can tell from the education and examination requirements mentioned previously, you must be very intelligent and a quick learner to be a successful Foreign Service officer. You should be flexible and adaptable to new cultures and traditions. You must be interested in the histories and traditions of foreign cultures and respectful of the practices of other nations. "Perhaps most important," James Prosser advises, "is a desire to communicate directly with foreign cultures and people. Start by learning their language and speak to them in it. That wins a lot of points in any discussion."

Good people skills are important because you will be expected to work as a member of a team and deal diplomatically with people from other countries. But, you will also be expected to work independently. You should be in good physical condition, so that your health can handle the climate variations of different countries.

EXPLORING

As a member of a foreign language club at your school, you may have the opportunity to visit other countries. If such programs do not exist, check with your school counselor or school librarian about discounted foreign travel packages available to student groups. Also, ask them about student exchange programs if you're interested in spending several weeks in another country. The People to People Student Ambassador Programs offer summer travel opportunities to students in grades five through 12. To learn about the expenses, destinations, and application process, visit the program's Web site (http://www.peopletopeople.com).

James Prosser's interest in foreign cultures started when he was very young. "Back in the 1930s," he says, "I built a crystal radio set, which enabled me to listen to distant radio stations. That led me to discover shortwave listening, and soon I was listening to foreign countries."

The American Foreign Service Association (AFSA), a professional association serving Foreign Service officers, publishes the *Foreign Service Journal* (http://www.afsa.org/fsj). The journal features articles by Foreign Service officers and academics that can give you insight into the Foreign Service.

It may be difficult finding part-time or summer jobs that are directly related to foreign service, but check with federal, state, and local government agencies and a local university. Some schools use volunteers or part-time employees to lead tours for foreign exchange students.

EMPLOYERS

The U.S. Department of State is the sole employer of Foreign Service officers. Foreign Service officers work in Washington, D.C., or are stationed in one of the more than 190 foreign countries that have U.S. embassies or consulates.

STARTING OUT

Many people apply to the Foreign Service directly after finishing graduate school, while others work in other government agencies or professions. Some serve with the Peace Corps or the military, gaining experience with foreign affairs before applying, or they work as teachers in American-sponsored schools overseas. Some work as congressional aides or interns. James Prosser joined the air force with hopes of being sent overseas. "In the back of my mind, I thought this enlistment would be my best opportunity to go abroad and experience foreign cultures." However, he was stationed within the United States for his entire four years with the air force. Near the end of his enlistment, one of his air force instructors suggested the Foreign Service.

Before being offered a job with the Foreign Service, you must pass the Foreign Service Officer Test. The exam consists of three multiple-choice sections that focus on general job knowledge, English expressions, and biographic information. There is also an essay that tests your knowledge of history, foreign policy, geography, and other relevant subjects. Registration for the test must be completed online at http://www.careers.state.gov/officer/register.html. At the time of registration, you must choose one of the five career tracks available with the Foreign Service: management affairs, consular affairs, economic affairs, political affairs, and public diplomacy. The U.S. State Department offers a study guide at its Web site to help applicants prepare for the exam. The number of positions available varies from year to year; typically, thousands of people apply for fewer than 100 positions. The Foreign Service has been known to cancel its annual exam because of too few job openings.

Those who pass the written exam move on to the oral interview and must pass a security clearance and a medical exam. But passing these tests doesn't necessarily mean employment; passing candidates are placed on a rank-order list based on their test scores. As jobs become available, offers are made to those at the top of the list.

ADVANCEMENT

New recruits are given a temporary appointment as career candidates, or junior officers. This probationary period lasts no longer than five years and consists of orientation and work overseas. During this time all junior officers must learn a foreign language. The candidate's performance will be reviewed after 36 months of service, at which time a decision on tenure (once tenured, an officer can't be separated from the service without written cause) and appointment as a career Foreign Service officer will be made. If tenure is not granted, the candidate will be reviewed again approximately one year later. Those who fail to show potential as career officers are dropped from the program.

Career officers are rated by their supervisors once a year. A promotion board decides who is eligible for advancement. Promotions are based on merit. A very experienced career officer may have the opportunity to serve as a member of the Senior Foreign Service, which involves directing, coordinating, and implementing U.S. foreign policy.

EARNINGS

Foreign Service officers are paid on a sliding scale. The exact figures depend on their qualifications and experience. According to the U.S. State Department, starting salaries for new appointees with no college experience and six or fewer years professional experience and those appointees with a bachelor's degree and no experience were $47,024 in 2010. Applicants who either had a master's or law degree, a bachelor's degree and six or more years professional experience, or no college degree but at least 12 years' professional experience earned $52,601 in 2010. Career officers earned base pay that ranged from $71,182 to $108,415 in 2010, while Senior Foreign Service officers made $119,554 to $179,700.

Benefits are usually generous, although they vary from post to post. Officers are housed free of charge or given a housing allowance. They receive a cost-of-living allowance, higher pay if they work in an area that imposes undue hardship on them, medical and retirement benefits, and an education allowance for their children.

Most officers overseas work regular hours. They may work more than 40 hours a week, though, because they are on call around the clock, seven days a week. Foreign Service officers receive paid vacation for anywhere from 13 to 26 days a year, depending on their length of service. They get three weeks of home leave for each year of duty overseas.

WORK ENVIRONMENT

Foreign Service officers may be assigned to work in Washington, D.C., or in any embassy or consulate in the world. They generally spend about 60 percent of their time abroad and are transferred every two to four years.

Foreign Service officers may serve tours of duty in such major world cities as London, Paris, Moscow, Tokyo, or in the less familiar locales of Madagascar, Nepal, or the Fiji Islands. Environments range from elegant and glamorous to remote and primitive.

Most offices overseas are clean, pleasant, and well equipped. But Foreign Service officers sometimes have to travel into areas that may present health hazards. Customs may differ considerably, medical care may be substandard or nonexistent, the climate may be extreme, or other hardships may exist. In some countries there is the danger of earthquakes, typhoons, or floods; in others, the danger of political upheaval or terrorist attacks.

Although embassy hours are normally the usual office hours of the host country, other tasks of the job may involve outside activities, such as attending or hosting dinners, lectures, public functions, or other necessary social engagements.

OUTLOOK

Many people view a career with the Foreign Service as an exciting and rewarding way to serve their country. As a result, there is heavy competition and extensive testing involved in obtaining Foreign Service positions. Only the most qualified people will land jobs as Foreign Service officers.

Nearly 265 U.S. embassies and consulates around the world are staffed by Foreign Service officers and specialists. While there will be continuing demand for Foreign Service officers, the number of workers is not expected to increase significantly during the next decade.

The Foreign Service seeks candidates who can manage programs and personnel, as well as experts in transnational issues, such as science and technology; the fight against diseases, such as AIDS; efforts to save the environment; antinarcotics efforts; and trade. The U.S. Department of State also has an increasing need for candidates with training and experience in administration and management of programs, economic policy issues, infrastructure, media relations, budgets, and human resources.

Those people interested in protecting diplomacy and the strength of the Foreign Service need to closely follow relevant legislation, as well as promote the importance of international affairs. "I personally believe," James Prosser says, "that retired Foreign Service officers have a duty to tell America what we are all about and how vital it is to the national interest that we continue to always have a complete and dedicated staff in the Foreign Service."

FOR MORE INFORMATION

This professional organization serving current and retired Foreign Service officers hosts an informative Web site and publishes career information, such as Inside a U.S. Embassy. *Read sections of the book online or contact*

American Foreign Service Association
2101 E Street, NW
Washington, DC 20037-2916
Tel: 800-704-2372
E-mail: afsa@afsa.org
http://www.afsa.org

The U.S. Department of State offers a wealth of information, including internship opportunities, the history of the Foreign Service, and current officers and embassies. Check out its Web site or contact

U.S. Department of State
2401 E Street, NW, Suite 518 H
Washington, DC 20522-0001
E-mail: careers@state.gov
http://careers.state.gov/officer

Fund-raisers

QUICK FACTS

School Subjects
Business
English
Mathematics

Personal Skills
Communication/ideas
Leadership/management

Work Environment
Primarily indoors
One location with some
travel

Minimum Education Level
Bachelor's degree

Salary Range
$20,000 to $61,000 to
$200,000+

Certification or Licensing
Voluntary

Outlook
About as fast as the average

DOT
293

GOE
N/A

NOC
N/A

O*NET-SOC
N/A

OVERVIEW

Political *fund-raisers* develop and coordinate the plans by which political candidates and organizations gain financial contributions, generate publicity, and fulfill fiscal objectives. Political fund-raisers are typically employed by politicians, political candidates, political party organizations, political consulting/fund-raising firms, and Political Action Committees (PACs).

HISTORY

For as long as there have been public elections in the world, political candidates have spent money in order to win. In the United States, the costs of political campaigns were not great enough to lend themselves to actual fund-raising until the early 1800s. By this time, various voting restrictions were eliminated and the country's population continued to grow. Both of these circumstances caused the number of potential voters to significantly increase. Political candidates now had a larger audience to reach, which would require more money. By the 1830s, the practice of regular solicitation of political donations had increased and continued to grow, with large corporate donations soon playing an important role. As time went on, political candidates were faced with national events that further increased the cost of campaigning, and thus the need for more fund-raising; women winning the right to vote in 1920 and the use of radio and television for campaigning after World War II are just two examples. The increased need for political campaigning money throughout history, and corporations' willingness to feed that need with large donations, created an environment in which corruption and abuse could occur. Campaign finance laws enacted in the 1920s, 1970s, and 2000s have largely affected today's methods of political fund-raising for contributions for individual candidates, political parties, or special-interest PACs. Today, anyone involved with political fund-raising must follow carefully all rules and regulations governing the process of raising money for political campaigns. Recent strategic developments in political fund-raising to counteract the dependence on large corporate donations include recognizing the importance of small contributions ($200 or less) from many individuals and successfully using the Internet for raising significant amounts of money.

THE JOB

Political fund-raising combines many different skills, such as financial management and accounting, public relations, marketing, human resources, management, and media communications. To be successful, the appeal for funds has to target the people most likely to donate, and donors have to be convinced of the good work being done by the politician or organization they are supporting. To do this, political fund-raisers need strong media support and savvy public relations. Political fund-raisers also have to bring people together, including volunteers, paid staff, political figures, and other community contacts, and direct them toward the common goal of raising money and supporting the political organization or candidate.

Political fund-raisers must identify potential donors for their candidate or organization. They must also identify the most effective and efficient ways of reaching these potential donors and securing a donation, preferably in the amount that is near or at the upper limit of what the donor can afford to contribute. Political fund-raisers must be aware of the diverse financial backgrounds of their many potential donors and try to find ways of successfully reaching out to all of them. Political fund-raisers do this in a number of ways, such as direct-mail appeals, telephone solicitations, Internet or e-mail appeals, and gatherings that serve to keep a political figure in the public eye while also raising money for his or her campaign. Gatherings take many shapes and forms, such as lavish dinners or parties where each donor contributes a significant amount of money—anywhere from hundreds to thousands of dollars—to mingle and perhaps be photographed with political candidates; or less expensive gatherings, such as an informal lunch or cocktail reception, where donors contribute perhaps less than $100 for the same privilege. The financial needs of most politicians and political organizations are so complex that a political fund-raiser may need to continually employ all of these methods to raise money for their candidate or organization, especially in the time prior to an election, when the need for money is great.

After each fund-raising appeal, a political fund-raiser must evaluate the success of the appeal. Did they reach their fund-raising goal? Was the appeal successful? What, if any factors detracted from the appeal? Did the actions of others involved with the appeal—such as public relations or marketing personnel, political party leaders, or the political candidate himself—help or hinder the fund-raising event? What factors and/or which individuals will be needed to guarantee similar or greater success for future appeals?

A political fund-raiser may spend a considerable amount of time with potential donors, volunteers, or other campaign staff via the phone; corresponding with them via letters, faxes or e-mail; and meeting with them in person. They also may spend much time on paperwork, as there is a great deal of it required with political contributions. A political fund-raiser must make sure that all of the necessary forms are completed and filed with the federal, state, and local governments in a timely manner.

Depending upon the experience of the political fund-raiser and the size of the campaign, organization, or firm that a political fund-raiser works for, they may be responsible for a specific task—like handling all direct-mail appeals, or being the liaison to all high-profile donors—or they may have many different responsibilities. During the course of a day, they may personally meet with an important donor, approve or reject a potential letter to be mailed to donors, touch base with the political candidate they are working for, sign off on plans for a fund-raising event, and train volunteers in tasks such as working the phones to solicit donations.

REQUIREMENTS

High School

To pursue a career in fund-raising, you should follow a college-preparatory curriculum. English, creative writing, speech, mathematics, business, political science, and history classes are recommended, as well as a foreign language, bookkeeping, and computer training. Extracurricular activities such as student council and community outreach programs can help you cultivate important leadership qualities and give you a taste of what fund-raising work requires.

Postsecondary Training
Fund-raising is not a curriculum taught in school, either in high school or at the university level. However, most political fund-raisers have earned at least a bachelor's degree. A broad liberal arts background, with special attention to political science, is a great benefit to political fund-raisers because of the nature of most fund-raising work. Specialized degrees that could benefit political fund-raisers include political science, communications, public relations, and business administration. Courses in economics, accounting, and mathematics are also very useful.

Certification or Licensing
CFRE International offers the certified fund raising executive designation to professionals who meet educational and experience requirements, pass a written examination, and pledge to uphold a code of ethics. This voluntary certification must be renewed every three years. Contact the organization for more information.

Other Requirements
Because political fund-raisers need to be able to talk and work with all kinds of people, you will need to be outgoing and friendly. Leadership is also an important quality, because you need to gain the respect of volunteers and inspire them to do their best. Their enthusiasm for a campaign can be a major factor in other people's commitment to the politician or political cause.

EXPLORING
The best way to gauge your interest in a political fund-raising career is to volunteer to assist with political fund-raising, such as for a local politician, political party, or political organization. When politicians and candidates are campaigning before an election, their organizations usually welcome as many volunteers as they can get. In this way, you can judge whether you enjoy this type of work. Try to maintain any networking contacts you make while volunteering, as they may be able to help you find a job at a later date.

If you are unable to volunteer in the political arena, you can still investigate fund-raising in general. Volunteer to help at religious organizations, social agencies, health charities, schools, and other organizations for their revenue drives. All of these groups tend to need volunteers and gladly welcome any help they can get. You will be able to observe the various efforts that go into a successful fund-raising drive and the work and dedication of professional fund-raisers.

EMPLOYERS

Political fund-raisers may be members of the staff of the political candidate or political organization in question. They may also be employed by fund-raising consulting firms, which for a fee will help political candidates or organizations manage their campaigns, budget their money and resources, determine the feasibility of different revenue programs, and counsel them in other ways. Most of these firms are partisan, that is, supporters of only one specific political party or organization.

STARTING OUT

The key to landing a job in political fund-raising is experience. Most organizations and firms prefer to hire fund-raisers who already have worked on other revenue drives. Because their time and budgets are limited, many organizations and firms are especially reluctant to hire people who need to be trained from scratch. Some small organizations that do not have a budget for hiring full-time fund-raisers may use volunteers.

Colleges offer many opportunities for experience, because nearly every college has at least one staff member (more than likely, an entire office) in charge of generating donations from alumni and other sources. These staff members will have useful advice to give on their profession, including private consulting firms that hire fund-raisers. A student may have to serve as a volunteer for such a firm first to get to know the people involved and be considered for a permanent position.

ADVANCEMENT

Political fund-raisers can advance to higher-paying jobs by gaining experience and developing skills. As responsibilities increase, fund-raisers may be put in charge of certain aspects of a campaign, such as the direct mail or corporate appeal, or may even direct an entire campaign. Promotions may also be determined by skill and creativity in handling difficult assignments. After gaining experience with several campaigns, some fund-raisers move on and start consulting businesses of their own, or they may move on to more prestigious political campaigns.

EARNINGS

The U.S. Department of Labor does not publish salary information for political fund-raisers. It is estimated that political fund-raisers earn starting salaries of less than $20,000. Although professionals generally start out with modest salaries, successful political fund-raisers can command significantly higher salaries—up to $200,000 or more. According to SimplyHired.com, in November 2010 the average salary for political fund-raisers working in Washington, D.C., was $61,000. Benefits for fund-raisers often are equivalent to other professional business positions, including paid vacation, group insurance plans, and paid sick days.

WORK ENVIRONMENT

The working conditions for political fund-raisers can sometimes be less than ideal. During election campaigning, they may have to work in temporary facilities. A certain amount of travel may be required if the political campaign affects a large geographical area. Their working hours can be irregular, because they have to meet and work with volunteers, potential donors, and other people whenever those people are available. When campaigns become intense, political fund-raisers may have to work long hours, seven days a week. With all the activity that goes on during a campaign, the atmosphere may become stressful, especially as elections and other deadlines draw near. So many demands are put on fund-raisers during a campaign—to arrange work schedules, meet with community groups, track finances, and so on—that they must be very organized, flexible, and committed to the overall strategy for the appeal.

OUTLOOK

The pressure for political candidates to raise enough money to fund expensive campaigns is now greater than ever, and so is the need for skilled political fund-raisers. Since there are so many fund-raising causes that will eagerly welcome volunteers, interested people should have no problem gaining experience, which should help lead them toward securing employment in the political arena.

FOR MORE INFORMATION

This organization provides professional guidance, assistance, and education to political consultants, including fund-raisers, and maintains a code of ethics.

American Association of Political Consultants
8400 Westpark Drive, 2nd Floor
McLean, VA 22102-5116
Tel: 703-245-8020
http://www.theaapc.org

For information on fund-raising careers, educational programs, and other resources, contact

Association of Fundraising Professionals
4300 Wilson Boulevard, Suite 300
Arlington, VA 22203-4179
Tel: 800-666-3863
http://www.afpnet.org

For comprehensive information on money in politics, visit the CRP Web site.

Center for Responsive Politics (CRP)
1101 14th Street, NW, Suite 1030
Washington, DC 20005-5635
Tel: 202-857-0044
E-mail: info@crp.org
http://www.opensecrets.org

For information on certification as a certified fund raising executive, contact

CFRE International
300 North Washington Street, Suite 504
Alexandria, VA 22314-2535
Tel: 703-820-5555
E-mail: info@cfre.org
http://www.cfre.org

Interpreters and Translators

OVERVIEW

An *interpreter* translates spoken passages of a foreign language into another specified language. The job is often designated by the language interpreted, such as Spanish or Japanese. In addition, many interpreters specialize according to subject matter. For example, *medical interpreters* have extensive knowledge of and experience in the health care field, while *court* or *judiciary interpreters* speak both a second language and the "language" of law. *Interpreters for the deaf*, also known as *sign language interpreters*, aid in communication between people who are unable to hear and those who can.

In contrast to interpreters, *translators* focus on written materials, such as books, plays, technical or scientific papers, legal documents, laws, treaties, and decrees. A *sight translator* performs a combination of interpreting and translating by reading printed material in one language while reciting it aloud in another.

There are approximately 50,900 interpreters and translators employed in the United States.

HISTORY

Until recently, most people who spoke two languages well enough to interpret and translate did so only on the side, working full time in some other occupation. For example, many diplomats and high-level government officials employed people who were able to serve as interpreters and translators, but only as needed. These employees spent the rest of their time assisting in other ways.

Interpreting and translating as full-time professions have emerged only recently, partly in response to the need for high-speed communication across the globe. The increasing use of complex diplomacy has also increased demand for full-time translating and interpreting professionals. For many years, diplomacy was practiced largely between just two nations. Rarely did conferences involve more than two languages at one time. The League of Nations, established by the Treaty of Versailles in 1919, established a new pattern of communication. Although the "language of diplomacy" was then considered to be French, diplomatic discussions were carried out in many different languages for the first time.

Since the early 1920s, multinational conferences have become commonplace. Trade and educational conferences are now held with participants of many nations in attendance. The United Nations (UN), which has been responsible for international diplomacy since the League of Nations dissolved, employs many full-time interpreters and translators. In addition, the European Union employs a large number of interpreters.

THE JOB

Although interpreters are needed for a variety of languages and different venues and circumstances, there are only two basic systems of interpretation: simultaneous and consecutive. Spurred in part by the invention and development of electronic sound equipment, simultaneous interpretation has been in use since the charter of the UN.

Simultaneous interpreters are able to convert a spoken sentence instantaneously. Some are so skilled that they are able to complete a sentence in the second language at almost the precise moment that the speaker is conversing in the original language. Such interpreters are usually familiar with the speaking habits of the speaker and can anticipate the way in which the sentence will be completed. The interpreter may also make judgments about the intent of the sentence or phrase from the speaker's gestures, facial expressions, and inflections. While working at a fast pace, the interpreter must be careful not to summarize, edit, or in any way change the meaning of what is being said.

In contrast, *consecutive interpreters* wait until the speaker has paused to convert speech into a second language. In this case, the speaker waits until the interpreter has finished before resuming the speech. Since every sentence is repeated in consecutive interpretation, this method takes longer than simultaneous interpretation.

In both systems, interpreters are placed so that they can clearly see and hear all that is taking place. In formal situations, such as those at the United Nations and other international conferences, interpreters are often assigned to a glass-enclosed booth. Speeches are transmitted to the booth, and interpreters, in turn, translate the speaker's words into a microphone. Each UN delegate can tune in the voice of the appropriate interpreter. Because of the difficulty of the job, these simultaneous interpreters usually work in pairs, each working 30-minute shifts.

All *international conference interpreters* are simultaneous interpreters. Many interpreters, however, work in situations other than formal diplomatic meetings. For example, interpreters are needed for negotiations of all kinds, as well as for legal, financial, medical, and business purposes. Court or judiciary interpreters, for example, work in courtrooms and at attorney-client meetings, depositions, and witness preparation sessions.

Other interpreters known as *guide* or *escort interpreters* serve on call, traveling with visitors from foreign countries who are touring the United States. Usually, these language specialists use consecutive interpretation. Their job is to make sure that whatever the visitors say is understood and that they also understand what is being said to them. Still other interpreters accompany groups of U.S. citizens on official tours abroad. On such assignments, they may be sent to any foreign country and might be away from the United States for long periods of time.

Interpreters also work on short-term assignments. Services may be required for only brief intervals, such as for a special conference or single interview with press representatives.

While interpreters focus on the spoken word, translators work with written language. They read and translate novels, plays, essays, nonfiction and technical works, legal documents, records and reports, speeches, and other written material. Translators generally follow a certain set of procedures in their work. They begin by reading the text, taking careful notes on what they do not understand. To translate questionable passages, they look up words and terms in specialized dictionaries and glossaries. They may also do additional reading on the subject to arrive at a better understanding. Finally, they write translated drafts in the target language.

Localization translation is a relatively new specialty. *Localization translators* adapt computer software, Web sites, and other business products for use in a different language or culture.

A sign language interpreter (*left*) conveys an elected official's speech to an audience. *(Peter Hvizdak, The Image Works)*

REQUIREMENTS

High School

If you are interested in becoming an interpreter or translator, you should take a variety of English courses, because most translating work is from a foreign language into English. The study of one or more foreign languages is vital. If you are interested in becoming proficient in one or more of the Romance languages, such as Italian, French, or Spanish, basic courses in Latin will be valuable.

While you should devote as much time as possible to the study of at least one foreign language, other helpful courses include speech, business, cultural studies, humanities, world history, geography, and political science. In fact, any course that emphasizes the written and/ or spoken word will be valuable to aspiring interpreters or translators. In addition, knowledge of a particular subject matter in which you may have interest, such as health, law, or science, will give you a professional edge if you want to specialize. Finally, courses in typing and word processing are recommended, especially if you want to pursue a career as a translator.

Postsecondary Training

Because interpreters and translators need to be proficient in grammar, have an excellent vocabulary in the chosen language, and have sound knowledge in a wide variety of subjects, employers generally require that applicants have at least a bachelor's degree. Scientific, conference, and localization interpreters are best qualified if they have graduate degrees.

In addition to language and field-specialty skills, you should take college courses that will allow you to develop effective techniques in public speaking, particularly if you're planning to pursue a career as an interpreter. Courses such as speech and debate will improve your diction and confidence as a public speaker.

Hundreds of colleges and universities in the United States offer degrees in languages. In addition, educational institutions now provide programs and degrees specialized for interpreting and translating. Georgetown University (http://www.georgetown.edu/learning.html) offers both undergraduate and graduate programs in languages and linguistics. Graduate degrees in interpretation and translation may be earned at the University of California at Santa Barbara (http://www.ucsb.edu) and the Monterey Institute of International Studies (http://www.miis.edu/academics). Many of these programs include both general and specialized courses, such as medical interpretation and legal translation.

Academic programs for the training of interpreters can be found in Europe as well. The University of Geneva's School of Translation and Interpretation (http://www.unige.ch/eti/index_en.html) is highly regarded among professionals in the field.

Certification or Licensing

Although interpreters and translators need not be certified to obtain jobs, employers often show preference to certified applicants. Certification in Spanish, Haitian Creole, and Navajo is also required for interpreters who are employed by federal courts. State and local courts often have their own specific certification requirements. The National Center for State Courts has more information on certification for these workers. Interpreters for the deaf who pass an examination may qualify for either comprehensive or legal certification that is offered by the National Association of the Deaf and the Registry of Interpreters for the Deaf.

The U.S. Department of State has a three-test requirement for interpreters. These tests include simple consecutive interpreting (escort), simultaneous interpreting (court/seminar), and conference-level interpreting (international conferences). Applicants must have several years of foreign language practice, advanced education in the language (preferably abroad), and be fluent in vocabulary for a very broad range of subjects.

Foreign language translators may be granted certification by the American Translators Association (ATA) upon successful completion of required exams. ATA certification is available for translators who translate the following languages into English: Arabic, Croatian, Danish, Dutch, French, German, Japanese, Portuguese, Russian, and Spanish. Certification is also available for translators who translate English into the following languages: Chinese, Croatian, Dutch, Finnish, French, German, Hungarian, Italian, Japanese, Polish, Russian, Spanish, and Ukrainian.

Court interpreters can become certified by the National Association of Judiciary Interpreters and Translators, and conference interpreters can become certified by the International Association of Conference Interpreters. Certification for medical interpreters is provided by the National Board of Certification for Medical Interpreters.

Other Requirements

Interpreters should be able to speak at least two languages fluently, without strong accents. They should be knowledgeable of not only the foreign language but also of the culture and social norms of the region or country in which it is spoken. Both interpreters and translators should read daily newspapers in the languages in which they work to keep current in both developments and usage.

Interpreters must have good hearing, a sharp mind, and a strong, clear, and pleasant voice. They must be able to be precise and quick in their translation. In addition to being flexible and versatile in their work, both interpreters and translators should have self-discipline and patience. Above all, they should have an interest in and love of language.

Finally, interpreters must be honest and trustworthy, observing any existing codes of confidentiality at all times. The ethical code of interpreters and translators is a rigid one. They must hold private proceedings in strict confidence. Ethics also demands that interpreters and translators not distort the meaning of the sentences that are spoken or written. No matter how much they may agree or disagree with the speaker or writer, interpreters and translators must be objective in their work. In addition, information they obtain in the process of interpretation or translation must never be passed along to unauthorized people or groups.

EXPLORING

If you have an opportunity to visit the United Nations, you can watch the proceedings to get some idea of the techniques and responsibilities of the job of the interpreter. Occasionally, an international conference session is televised, and the work of the interpreters can be observed. You should note, however, that interpreters who work at these conferences are in the top positions of the vocation. Not everyone may aspire to such jobs. The work of interpreters and translators is usually less public, but not necessarily less interesting.

If you have adequate skills in a foreign language, you might consider traveling in a country in which the language is spoken. If you can converse easily and without a strong accent and can interpret to others who may not understand the language well, you may have what it takes to work as an interpreter or translator.

For any international field, it is important that you familiarize yourself with other cultures. You can even arrange to regularly correspond with a pen pal in a foreign country. You may also want to join a school club that focuses on a particular language, such as the French Club or the Spanish Club. If no such clubs exist, consider forming one. Student clubs can allow you to hone your foreign language speaking and writing skills and learn about other cultures.

Finally, participating on a speech or debate team can allow you to practice your public speaking skills, increase your confidence, and polish your overall appearance by working on eye contact, gestures, facial expressions, tone, and other elements used in public speaking.

EMPLOYERS

There are approximately 50,900 interpreters and translators in the United States. Although many interpreters and translators work for government or international agencies, some are employed by private firms. Large import-export companies often have interpreters or translators on their payrolls, although these employees generally perform additional duties for the firm. International banks, companies, organizations, and associations often employ both interpreters and translators to facilitate communication. In addition, translators and interpreters work at publishing houses, schools, bilingual newspapers, radio and television stations, airlines, shipping companies, law firms, and scientific and medical operations.

While translators are employed nationwide, a large number of interpreters find work in New York and Washington, D.C. Among the largest employers of interpreters and translators are the United Nations, the World Bank, the U.S. Department of State, the Bureau of the Census, the CIA, the FBI, the Library of Congress, the Red Cross, the YMCA, and the armed forces.

Finally, many interpreters and translators work independently in private practice. These self-employed professionals must be disciplined and driven, since they must handle all aspects of the business such as scheduling work and billing clients.

STARTING OUT

Most interpreters and translators begin as part-time freelancers until they gain experience and contacts in the field. Individuals can apply for jobs directly to the hiring firm, agency, or organization. Many of these employers advertise available positions in the classified section of the newspaper or on the Internet. In addition, contact your college's career services office and language department to inquire about job leads.

While many opportunities exist, top interpreting and translating jobs are hard to obtain since the competition for these higher profile positions is fierce. You may be wise to develop supplemental skills that can be attractive to employers while refining your interpreting and translating techniques. The UN, for example, employs administrative assistants who can take shorthand and transcribe notes in two or more languages. The UN also hires tour guides who speak more than one language. Such positions can be initial steps toward your future career goals.

ADVANCEMENT

Competency in language determines the speed of advancement for interpreters and translators. Job opportunities and promotions are plentiful for those who have acquired great proficiency in languages. However, interpreters and translators need to constantly work and study to keep abreast of the changing linguistic trends for a given language. The constant addition of new vocabulary for technological advances, inventions, and processes keep languages fluid. Those who do not keep up with changes will find that their communication skills become quickly outdated.

Interpreters and translators who work for government agencies advance by clearly defined grade promotions. Those who work for other organizations can aspire to become chief interpreters or chief translators, or *reviewers* who check the work of others.

Although advancement in the field is generally slow, interpreters and translators will find many opportunities to succeed as freelancers. Some can even establish their own bureaus or agencies.

EARNINGS

Earnings for interpreters and translators vary, depending on experience, skills, number of languages used, and employers. In the federal government, trainee interpreters and translators generally begin at the GS-5 rating, earning from $27,431 to $35,657 a year in 2010. Those with a college degree can start at the higher GS-7 level, earning from $33,979 to $44,176. With an advanced degree, trainees begin at the GS-9 ($41,563 to $54,028), GS-10 ($45,771 to $59,505), or GS-11 level ($50,287 to $65,371). Those who were employed in local government in 2009 earned mean annual salaries of $45,070, according to the U.S. Department of Labor (DOL). The DOL reports salaries ranging from less than $22,810 to more than $74,150 for interpreters and translators.

Interpreters who are employed by the United Nations work under a salary structure called the Common System. In 2008, UN short-term interpreters (workers employed for a duration of 60 days or less) had daily gross pay of $563.50 (Grade I) or $368.50 (Grade II). UN short-term translators and revisers had daily gross pay of $209.00 (Translator I), $256.40 (Translator II), $303.60 (Translator III/Reviser I), $342.50 (Translator IV/Reviser II), or $381.50 (Reviser III).

Interpreters and translators who work on a freelance basis usually charge by the word, the page, the hour, or the project. Freelance interpreters for international conferences or meetings can earn between $300 and $500 a day from the U.S. government.

By the hour, freelance translators usually earn between $15 and $35; however, rates vary depending on the language and the subject matter. Book translators work under contract with publishers. These contracts cover the fees that are to be paid for translating work as well as royalties, advances, penalties for late payments, and other provisions.

Interpreters and translators working in a specialized field have high earning potential. According to the National Association of Judiciary Interpreters and Translators, the federal courts paid $376 per day for certified or professionally qualified court interpreters in 2008. Most work as freelancers, earning annual salaries from $30,000 to $100,000 a year.

Interpreters who work for the deaf also may work on a freelance basis, earning anywhere from $12 to $40 an hour, according to the Registry of Interpreters for the Deaf. Those employed with an agency, government organization, or school system can earn up to $30,000 to start; in urban areas, $40,000 to $50,000 a year.

Depending on the employer, interpreters and translators often enjoy such benefits as health and life insurance, pension plans, and paid vacation and sick days.

WORK ENVIRONMENT

Interpreters and translators work under a wide variety of circumstances and conditions. As a result, most do not have typical nine-to-five schedules.

Conference interpreters probably have the most comfortable physical facilities in which to work. Their glass-enclosed booths are well lit and temperature controlled. Court or judiciary interpreters work in courtrooms or conference rooms, while interpreters for the deaf work at educational institutions as well as a wide variety of other locations.

Interpreters who work for escort or tour services are often required to travel for long periods of time. Their schedules are dictated by the group or person for whom they are interpreting. A freelance interpreter may work out of one city or be assigned anywhere in the world as needed.

Translators usually work in offices, although many spend considerable time in libraries and research centers. Freelance translators often work at home, using their own personal computers, the Internet, dictionaries, and other resource materials.

While both interpreting and translating require flexibility and versatility, interpreters in particular, especially those who work for international congresses or courts, may experience considerable stress and fatigue. Knowing that a great deal depends upon their absolute accuracy in interpretation can be a weighty responsibility.

OUTLOOK

Employment opportunities for interpreters and translators are expected to grow much faster than the average for all careers through 2018, according to the DOL. However, competition for available positions will be fierce. With the explosion of such technologies as the Internet, lightning-fast Internet connections, and videoconferencing, global communication has taken great strides. In short, the world has become smaller, so to speak, creating a demand for professionals to aid in the communication between people of different languages and cultural backgrounds.

In addition to new technological advances, demographic factors will fuel demand for translators and interpreters. Although some immigrants who come to the United States assimilate easily with respect to culture and language, many have difficulty learning English. As immigration to the United States continues to increase, interpreters and translators will be needed to help immigrants function in an English-speaking society. According to Ann Macfarlane, former president of the American Translators Association, "community interpreting" for immigrants and refugees is a challenging area requiring qualified language professionals.

Another demographic factor influencing the interpreting and translating fields is the growth in overseas travel. Americans on average are spending an increasing amount of money on travel, especially to foreign countries. The resulting growth of the travel industry will create a need for interpreters to lead tours, both at home and abroad.

In addition to leisure travel, business travel is spurring the need for more translators and interpreters. With workers traveling abroad in growing numbers to attend meetings, conferences, and seminars with overseas clients, interpreters and translators will be needed to help bridge both the language and cultural gaps.

While no more than a few thousand interpreters and translators are employed in the largest markets (the federal government and international organizations), other job options exist. The medical field, for example, will provide many jobs for language professionals, translating such products as pharmaceutical inserts, research papers, and medical reports for insurance companies. There will also be strong demand for interpreters in health care settings such as hospitals, outpatient treatment centers, and large offices of physicians due to the steady increase in immigrants to the United States who do not speak English as their primary language. Opportunities exist for qualified individuals in law, trade and business, tourism, recreation, and the government (including homeland security; interpreters and translators who are fluent in Arabic, Azerbaijani, Chinese, Estonian, Georgian, Hebrew, Italian, Japanese, Kurdish, and other languages of limited diffusion will have especially strong employment opportunities).

The DOL predicts that employment growth will be limited for conference interpreters and literary translators.

FOR MORE INFORMATION

For information on careers in literary translation, contact
American Literary Translators Association
University of Texas–Dallas
800 West Campbell Road, Mail Station JO51
Richardson, TX 75080-3021

Tel: 972-883-2092
http://www.utdallas.edu/alta

For more on the translating and interpreting professions, including information on accreditation, contact
American Translators Association
225 Reinekers Lane, Suite 590
Alexandria, VA 22314-2875
Tel: 703-683-6100
E-mail: ata@atanet.org
http://www.atanet.org

For information on medical interpreting and certification, contact
International Medical Interpreters Association
800 Washington Street, Box 271
Boston, MA 02111-1845
Tel: 617-636-1798
E-mail: info@imiaweb.org
http://www.imiaweb.org

For more information on court interpreting and certification, contact
National Association of Judiciary Interpreters and Translators
1707 L Street, NW, Suite 507
Washington, DC 20036-4201
Tel: 202-293-0342
http://www.najit.org

For information on health care interpreting, contact
National Council on Interpreting in Health Care
5505 Connecticut Avenue, NW, #119
Washington, DC 20015-2601
Tel: 202-596-2436
E-mail: info@NCIHC.org
http://www.ncihc.org

For information on interpreter training programs for working with the deaf and certification, contact
Registry of Interpreters for the Deaf Inc.
333 Commerce Street
Alexandria, VA 22314-2801
Tel: 703-838-0030
http://www.rid.org

For information on union membership for freelance interpreters and translators, contact

Translators and Interpreters Guild
PO Box 77624
Washington, DC 20013-8624
Tel: 202-684-3324
E-mail: unionlanguages@aol.com
http://www.unionlanguages.org

For information on opportunities with the federal government, contact

U.S. Department of State
Office of Language Services
2401 E Street, NW, SA-1, 14th Floor
Washington, DC 20522-0001
Tel: 202-261-8800
http://languageservices.state.gov

Lawyers and Judges

QUICK FACTS

School Subjects
English
Government
Speech

Personal Skills
Communication/ideas
Leadership/management

Work Environment
Primarily indoors
Primarily multiple locations

Minimum Education Level
Law degree

Salary Range
$55,270 to $113,240 to
  $1,000,000+ (lawyers)
$33,130 to $112,830 to
  $218,237 (judges)

Certification or Licensing
Required by all states

Outlook
About as fast as the average
  (lawyers)
More slowly than the
  average (judges)

DOT
110 (lawyers)
111 (judges)

GOE
04.02.01

NOC
4112 (lawyers)
4111 (judges)

O*NET-SOC
23-1011.00 (lawyers)
23-1021.00, 23-1023.00
  (judges)

OVERVIEW

Lawyers, or *attorneys*, serve in two ways in our legal system: as advocates and as advisers. As advocates, they represent the rights of their clients in trials and depositions or in front of administrative and government bodies. As advisers, attorneys counsel clients on how the law affects business or personal decisions, such as the purchase of property or the creation of a will. Lawyers represent individuals, businesses, and corporations. Approximately 759,200 lawyers work in the United States today, in various areas of the profession.

Judges are elected or appointed officials who preside over federal, state, county, and municipal courts. They apply the law to citizens and businesses and oversee court proceedings according to the established law. Judges also give new rulings on issues not previously decided. Approximately 51,200 judges work in all levels of the judiciary arm of the United States.

HISTORY

The tradition of governing people by laws has been established over centuries. Societies have built up systems of law that have been studied and drawn upon by later governments. The earliest known law is the Code of Hammurabi, developed about 1800 B.C. by the ruler of the Sumerians. Another early set of laws was the Law of Moses, known as the Ten Commandments. Every set of laws, no matter when they were introduced, has been accompanied by the need for someone to explain those laws and help others live under them.

The great orators of ancient Greece and Rome set up schools for young boys to learn by apprenticeship the many skills involved in pleading a law case. To be an eloquent speaker was the greatest

Texas Supreme Court Chief Justice Wallace Jefferson signs documents in his chambers. *(Bob Daemmrich, The Image Works)*

advantage. The legal profession has matured since those earlier times; a great deal of training and an extensive knowledge of legal matters are required of the modern lawyer and judge.

Much modern European law was organized and refined by legal experts assembled by Napoleon; their body of law was known as the Napoleonic Code. English colonists coming to America brought English common law, from which American laws have grown. In areas of the United States that were heavily settled by Spanish colonists, there are traces of Spanish law. As the population in the country grew, along with business, those who knew the law were in high demand. The two main kinds of law are *civil* and *criminal*, but many other specialty areas are also prevalent today. When our country was young, most lawyers were general law practitioners—they knew and worked with all the laws for their clients' sakes. Today, there are many more lawyers who specialize in areas such as tax law, corporate law, and intellectual property law.

THE JOB

All lawyers may give legal advice and represent clients in court when necessary. No matter what their specialty, their job is to help clients know their rights under the law and then help them achieve these rights before a judge, jury, government agency, or other legal forum, such as an arbitration panel. Lawyers may represent businesses and individuals. For businesses, they manage tax matters, arrange for stock to be issued, handle claims cases, represent the firm in real estate dealings, and advise on all legal matters. For individuals they may be trustees, guardians, or executors; they may draw up wills or contracts or advise on income taxes or on the purchase or sale of a home. Some work solely in the courts; others carry on most of their business outside of court, doing such tasks as drawing up mortgages, deeds, contracts, and other legal documents or by handling the background work necessary for court cases, which might include researching cases in a law library or interviewing witnesses. A number of lawyers work to establish and enforce laws for the federal and state governments by drafting legislation, representing the government in court, or serving as judges.

Lawyers can also take positions as *professors* in law schools. Administrators, research workers, and writers are also important to the profession. Administrative positions in business or government may be of a nonlegal nature, but the qualities, background, and experience of a lawyer are often helpful in such positions.

Other individuals with legal training may choose not to practice but instead opt for careers in which their background and knowledge of law are important. These careers include tax collectors, credit investigators, FBI agents, insurance adjusters, process servers, and probation officers.

Some of the specialized fields for lawyers are described in the following paragraphs.

Civil lawyers work in a field also known as private law. They focus on damage suits and breach-of-contract suits; prepare and draw up deeds, leases, wills, mortgages, and contracts; and act as trustees, guardians, or executors of an estate when necessary.

Criminal lawyers, also known as *defense lawyers*, specialize in cases dealing with offenses committed against society or the state, such as theft, murder, or arson. They interview clients and witnesses to ascertain facts in a case, correlate their findings with known cases, and prepare a case to defend a client against the charges made. They conduct a defense at the trial, examine witnesses, and summarize the case with a closing argument to a jury.

District attorneys, also known as *prosecuting attorneys*, represent the city, county, state, or federal government in court proceedings. They gather and analyze evidence and review legal material relevant to a lawsuit. Then they present their case to the grand jury, which decides whether the evidence is sufficient for an indictment. If it is not, the suit is dismissed and there is no trial. If the grand jury decides to indict the accused, however, the case goes to court, where the district attorney appears before the judge and jury to present evidence against the defendant.

Probate lawyers specialize in planning and settling estates. They draw up wills, deeds of trust, and similar documents for clients who want to plan for giving their belongings to their heirs when they die. Upon a client's death, probate lawyers vouch for the validity of the will and represent the executors and administrators of the estate.

Bankruptcy attorneys assist their clients, both individuals and corporations, in obtaining protection from creditors under existing bankruptcy laws and with financial reorganization and debt repayment.

Corporation lawyers, sometimes known as *corporate lawyers*, advise corporations concerning their legal rights, obligations, or privileges. They study constitutions, statutes, previous decisions, ordinances, and decisions of quasi-judicial bodies that are applicable to corporations. They advise corporations on the pros and cons of prosecuting or defending a lawsuit. They act as agent of the corporation in various transactions and seek to keep clients from expensive litigation.

Maritime lawyers, sometimes referred to as *admiralty lawyers*, specialize in laws regulating commerce and navigation on the high seas and any navigable waters, including inland lakes and rivers. Although there is a general maritime law, it operates in each country according to that country's courts, laws, and customs. Maritime law covers contracts, insurance, property damage, and personal injuries.

Intellectual property lawyers focus on helping their clients with patents, trademarks, and copyright protection. *Patent lawyers* are intellectual property lawyers who specialize in securing patents for inventors from the United States Patent Office and prosecuting or defending suits of patent infringements. They prepare detailed specifications for the patent, may organize a corporation, or advise an existing corporation to commercialize on a patent. Biotechnology patent law is a further specialization of patent law. *Biotechnology patent lawyers* specialize in helping biotechnology researchers, scientists, and research corporations with all legal aspects of their biotechnology patents.

Elder law attorneys are lawyers who specialize in providing legal services for the elderly and, in some cases, the disabled.

Tax attorneys handle cases resulting from problems of inheritance, income tax, estate tax, franchises, and real estate tax, among other things.

Insurance attorneys advise insurance companies about legal matters pertaining to insurance transactions. They approve the wording of insurance policies, review the legality of claims against the company, and draw up legal documents.

An *international lawyer* specializes in the body of rules that are observed by nations in their relations with one another. Some of these laws have been agreed to in treaties, some have evolved from long-standing customs and traditions.

Securities and exchange lawyers monitor individuals and corporations involved in trading and oversee their activities to make sure they comply with applicable laws. When corporations undergo takeovers and mergers, securities and exchange lawyers are there to represent the corporations' interests and fulfill all legal obligations involved in the transaction.

Real estate lawyers handle the transfer of property and perform such duties as searching public records and deeds to establish titles of property, holding funds for investment in escrow accounts, and acting as trustees of property. They draw up legal documents and act as agents in various real estate transactions.

Title attorneys deal with titles, leases, contracts, and other legal documents pertaining to the ownership of land, and gas, oil, and mineral rights. They prepare documents to cover the purchase or sale of such property and rights, examine documents to determine ownership, advise organizations about legal requirements concerning titles, and participate in the trial or lawsuits in connection with titles.

Other lawyers may specialize in environmental, employee benefits, entertainment, or health law.

It is important to note that once you are licensed to practice law, you are legally qualified to practice any one or more of these and many other specialties. Some general practitioners handle both criminal and civil matters of all sorts. To become licensed, you must be admitted to the bar of the state in which you plan to practice. Bar examiners test the qualifications of applicants. They prepare and administer written exams covering legal subjects, examine candidates orally, and recommend admission of those who meet the prescribed standards.

Lawyers become judges by either election or appointment, and preside over federal, state, county, or municipal courts. Judges administer court procedures during trials and hearings and establish new rules on questions where standard procedures have not previously been set. They read or listen to claims made by parties involved in civil suits and make decisions based on facts, applicable statutes, and prior court decisions. They examine evidence in criminal cases to see if it supports the charges. Judges listen to the presentation of cases, rule on the admission of evidence and testimony, and settle disputes between attorneys. They instruct juries on their duties and advise them of laws that apply to the case. They sentence defendants found guilty of criminal charges and decide who is responsible in nonjury civil cases. Besides their work in the courtroom, judges also research legal matters, study prior rulings, write opinions, and keep abreast of legislation that may affect their rulings.

Some judges have other titles such as *magistrate*, or *justice*, and preside over a limited jurisdiction. Magistrates hear civil cases in which damages do not exceed a prescribed maximum, as well as minor misdemeanor cases that do not involve penitentiary sentences or fines that exceed a certain specified amount.

REQUIREMENTS

High School

A high school diploma, a college degree, and three years of law school are minimum requirements for a law degree. A high school diploma is a first step on the ladder of education that a lawyer must climb. If you are considering a career in law, courses such as government, history, social studies, and economics provide a solid background for entering college-level courses. Speech courses are also helpful to build strong communication skills necessary for the profession. Also take advantage of any computer-related classes or experience you can get, because lawyers and judges often use technology to research and interpret the law, from surfing the Internet to searching legal databases.

Postsecondary Training
To enter any law school approved by the American Bar Association, you must satisfactorily complete at least three, and usually four, years of college work. Most law schools do not specify any particular courses for prelaw education. Usually a liberal arts track is most advisable, with courses in English, history, economics, social sciences, logic, and public speaking. A college student planning on specialization in a particular area of law, however, might also take courses significantly related to that area, such as economics, agriculture, or political science. Those interested should contact several law schools to learn more about any requirements and to see if they will accept credits from the college the student is planning to attend.

Currently, 200 law schools in the United States are approved by the American Bar Association; others, many of them night schools, are approved by state authorities only. Most of the approved law schools, however, do have night sessions to accommodate part-time students. Part-time courses of study usually take four years.

Law school training consists of required courses such as legal writing and research, contracts, criminal law, constitutional law, torts, and property. The second and third years may be devoted to specialized courses of interest to the student, such as evidence, business transactions and corporations, or admiralty. The study of cases and decisions is of basic importance to the law student, who will be required to read and study thousands of these cases. A degree of juris doctor (J.D.) or bachelor of laws (LL.B.) is usually granted upon graduation. Some law students considering specialization, research, or teaching may go on for advanced study.

Most law schools require that applicants take the Law School Admission Test (LSAT), where prospective law students are tested on their critical thinking, writing, and reasoning abilities.

Certification or Licensing
Every state requires that lawyers be admitted to the bar of that state before they can practice. They require that applicants graduate from an approved law school and that they pass a written examination in the state in which they intend to practice. In a few states, graduates

of law schools within the state are excused from these written examinations. After lawyers have been admitted to the bar in one state, they can practice in another state without taking a written examination if the states have reciprocity agreements; however, they will be required to meet certain state standards of good character and legal experience and pay any applicable fees.

Other Requirements

Federal courts and agencies have their own rules regulating admission to practice. Other requirements vary among the states. For example, the states of Vermont, New York, Washington, Virginia, California, Maine, and Wyoming allow a person who has spent several years reading law in a law office but has no college training or who has a combination of reading and law school experience to take the state bar examination. Few people now enter law practice in this manner.

A few states accept the study of law by correspondence. Some states require that newly graduated lawyers serve a period of clerkship in an established law firm before they are eligible to take the bar examination.

Almost all judges appointed or elected to any court must be lawyers and members of the bar, usually with many years of experience.

Both lawyers and judges have to be effective communicators, work well with people, and be able to find creative solutions to problems, such as complex court cases.

EXPLORING

If you think a career as a lawyer or judge might be right up your alley, there are several ways you can find out more about it before making that final decision. First, sit in on a trial or two at your local or state courthouse. Try to focus mainly on the judge and the lawyer and take note of what they do. Write down questions you have and terms or actions you do not understand. Then, talk to your school counselor and ask for help in setting up a telephone or in-person interview with a judge or lawyer. Ask questions and get the scoop on what those careers are really all about. Also, talk to your counselor or political science teacher about starting or joining a job-shadowing program. Job-shadowing programs allow you to follow a person in a certain career around for a day or two to get an idea of what goes on in a typical day. You may even be invited to help out with a few minor duties.

You can also search the Internet for general information about lawyers and judges and current court cases. Read court transcripts and summary opinions written by judges on issues of importance today. Visit the Web sites of professional associations and organizations. Here are a few suggestions: American Bar Association: Career Counsel (http://www.abanet.org/careercenter), American Bar Association: How Courts Work (http://www.abanet.org/publiced/courts/home.html), American Bar Association: Pre-Law Toolkit (http://www.abanet.org/careercounsel/prelaw), and Law School Admission Council: Getting Started (http://www.lsac.org/jd/default.asp).

After you have done some research and talked to a lawyer or judge and you still think you are destined for law school, try to get a part-time job in a law office. Ask your counselor for help.

If you are already in law school, you might consider becoming a student member of the American Bar Association. Student members receive *Student Lawyer*, a magazine that contains useful information for aspiring lawyers. Sample articles from the magazine can be read at http://www.abanet.org/lsd/studentlawyer.

EMPLOYERS

Approximately 759,200 lawyers are employed in the United States. About 75 percent of them work in private practice, either in law firms or alone. The others are employed in government, often at the local level. Lawyers working for the federal government hold positions in the Departments of Justice, Treasury, and Defense. Lawyers also hold positions as house counsel for public utilities, transportation companies, banks, insurance companies, real estate agencies, manufacturing firms, welfare and religious organizations, and other businesses and nonprofit organizations.

Approximately 51,200 judges are employed in the United States. Judges and magistrates work for federal, state, and local levels of government. About 26 percent of all judges work for state and local governments.

STARTING OUT

The first steps in entering the law profession are graduation from an approved law school and passing a state bar examination. Usually beginning lawyers do not go into solo practice right away. It is often difficult to become established, and additional experience is helpful to the beginning lawyer. Also, most lawyers do not specialize in a particular branch of law without first gaining experience. Beginning lawyers usually work as assistants to experienced lawyers. At first they do mainly research and routine work. After a few years of successful experience, they may be ready to go out on their own. Other choices open to the beginning lawyer include joining an established law firm or entering into partnership with another lawyer. Positions are also available with banks, business corporations, insurance companies, private utilities, and with a number of government agencies at different levels.

Many new lawyers are recruited by law firms or other employers directly from law school. Recruiters come to the school and interview possible hires. Other new graduates can get job leads from local and state bar associations.

ADVANCEMENT

Lawyers with outstanding ability can expect to go a long way in their profession. Novice lawyers generally start as law clerks, but as they prove themselves and develop their abilities, many opportunities for advancement will arise. They may be promoted to junior partner in a law firm or establish their own practice. Lawyers may enter politics and become judges, mayors, congressmen, or other government leaders. Top positions are available in business, too, for the qualified lawyer. Lawyers working for the federal government advance according to the civil service system. Judges usually advance from lower courts to higher courts either in terms of the matters that are decided or in terms of the level—local, state, or federal.

EARNINGS

Incomes generally increase as the lawyer gains experience and becomes better known in the field. The beginning lawyer in solo practice may barely make ends meet for the first few years. According to the National Association for Law Placement, 2009 mean salaries for new lawyers were $130,000. New lawyers hired at firms with two to 10 attorneys received median starting salaries of $40,000 to $65,000, while those employed by large firms with 501 or more workers were paid $160,000.

Experienced lawyers earn salaries that vary depending on the type, size, and location of their employers. According to the U.S. Department of Labor, the 2009 median salary for practicing lawyers was $113,240, although some senior partners earned well over $1 million a year. Ten percent earned less than $55,270. General attorneys in the federal government received $127,550 in 2009. State and local government attorneys generally made less, earning $82,750 and $91,040, respectively, in 2009.

Judges earned median annual salaries of $112,830 in 2009, according to the U.S. Department of Labor. Salaries ranged from less than $33,130 to more than $166,400.

According to the Administrative Office of the U.S. Courts, federal district court judges earned an average of $169,300 in 2008. The chief justice of the United States Supreme Court earned $217,400, while associate justices of the Supreme Court earned $208,100 in 2008. A survey conducted by the National Center for State Courts reports that 2009 average salaries for associate judges in the states' highest courts ranged from $112,530 to $218,237. Judges serving in intermediate appellate courts earned salaries that ranged from $105,050 to $204,599, and in general jurisdiction trial courts, salaries ranged from $104,170 to $178,789.

Lawyers and judges usually receive paid vacations and holidays, sick leave, hospitalization and insurance benefits, and pension programs. Some employers also offer profit-sharing plans. Lawyers who have their own firms must provide their own benefits.

WORK ENVIRONMENT

Offices and courtrooms are usually pleasant, although busy, places to work. Lawyers also spend significant amounts of time in law libraries or record rooms, in the homes and offices of clients, and sometimes in the jail cells of clients or prospective witnesses. Many lawyers never work in a courtroom. Unless they are directly involved in litigation, they may never perform at a trial.

Some courts, such as small claims, family, or surrogate, may have evening hours to provide flexibility to the community. Criminal arraignments may be held at any time of the day or night. Court hours for most lawyers and judges are usually regular business hours, with a one-hour lunch break. Often lawyers have to work long hours, spending evenings and weekends preparing cases and materials and working with clients. In addition to the work, the lawyer must always keep up with the latest developments in the profession. Also, it takes a long time to become a qualified lawyer, and it may be difficult to earn an adequate living until the lawyer gets enough experience to develop an established private practice.

Lawyers who are employed at law firms must often work grueling hours to advance in the firm. Spending long weekend hours doing research and interviewing people should be expected.

OUTLOOK

According to the *Occupational Outlook Handbook*, employment for lawyers is expected to grow about as fast as the average for all careers through 2018, but high numbers of law school graduates have created strong competition for jobs. Continued population growth, typical business activities, and increased numbers of legal cases involving health care, antitrust, environmental, intellectual property, international law, venture capital, energy, corporate and security litigation, elder law, and sexual harassment issues, among others, will create a steady demand for lawyers. Law services will be more accessible to the middle-income public with the popularity of prepaid legal services and clinics. However, stiff competition has and will continue to urge some lawyers to look outside the legal profession for employment. Administrative and managerial positions in real-estate companies, banks, insurance firms, and government agencies are typical areas where legal training is useful.

The top 10 percent of the graduating students of the country's best law schools will have more opportunities with well-known law firms and corporations, in government agencies, and in law schools in the next few decades. Lawyers in solo practice will find it hard to earn a living until their practice is fully established. The best opportunities exist in small towns or suburbs of large cities, where there is less competition and new lawyers can meet potential clients more easily.

Graduates with lower class rankings and from lesser-known schools may have difficulty in obtaining the most desirable positions.

Employment of judges is expected to grow more slowly than the average through 2018. Budgetary cuts will limit the hiring of new judges—especially at the federal level. There will be some employment growth as a result of demographic shifts in the U.S. population; more judges will be needed to handle immigration- and elder law-related issues. Demand for judges should grow as the public focuses more on crime, as well as seeks to settle disputes that were previously handled out of court to court. Developments in medical science, electronic commerce, information technology, and globalization have also created new opportunities for judges, as well as increased the complexity of their work. Most positions will open as judges retire or leave the field to go into the private sector (which is more lucrative). There may be an increase in judges in cities with large population growth, but competition will be high for any openings.

FOR MORE INFORMATION

For information about law student services offered by the ABA, contact

American Bar Association (ABA)
321 North Clark Street
Chicago, IL 60654-7598

Tel: 800-285-2221
E-mail: askaba@abanet.org
http://www.abanet.org

This is a professional membership organization for judges in the United States and its territories (Puerto Rico, Guam, American Samoa, and the Virgin Islands), Canada, and Mexico. It offers an essay contest for law students.
American Judges Association
300 Newport Avenue
Williamsburg, VA 23185-4147
Tel: 757-259-1841
E-mail: aja@ncsc.dni.us
http://aja.ncsc.dni.us

For information on AALS member schools and workshops and seminars, contact
Association of American Law Schools (AALS)
1201 Connecticut Avenue, NW, Suite 800
Washington, DC 20036-2717
Tel: 202-296-8851
E-mail: aals@aals.org
http://www.aals.org

The FBA provides information for lawyers and judges involved in federal practice.
Federal Bar Association (FBA)
1220 North Fillmore Street, Suite 444
Arlington, VA 22201-6501
Tel: 571-481-9100
E-mail: fba@fedbar.org
http://www.fedbar.org

Contact the Federal Judicial Center for information about educational programs for federal judges. Visit its Web site to read biographies of federal judges since 1789, landmark judicial legislation, and histories of individual U.S. courts.
Federal Judicial Center
Thurgood Marshall Federal Judiciary Building
One Columbus Circle, NE
Washington DC 20002-8003
Tel: 202-502-4000
http://www.fjc.gov

*For information on the Law School Admission Test and choosing
and paying for law school, contact*
Law School Admission Council
662 Penn Street
Newtown, PA 18940-2176
Tel: 215-968-1001
http://www.lsac.org

*For information on choosing a law school, law careers, salaries, and
alternative law careers, contact*
National Association for Law Placement
1025 Connecticut Avenue, NW, Suite 1110
Washington, DC 20036-5413
Tel: 202-835-1001
E-mail: info@nalp.org
http://www.nalp.org

*This is a professional organization for female judges, judicial clerks,
attorneys, and law students. Male law professionals are also invited
to become members. It offers scholarships and internships to law
students.*
National Association of Women Judges
E-mail: nawj@nawj.org
http://www.nawj.org

*This professional organization for both female and male lawyers
offers career development programs for new lawyers, publications,
a mentorship program, and membership for law students.*
National Association of Women Lawyers
American Bar Center
321 North Clark Street, MS 15.2
Chicago, IL 60654-4714
Tel: 312-988-6186
E-mail: nawl@nawl.org
http://www.nawl.org

For information on state courts, contact
National Center for State Courts
300 Newport Avenue
Williamsburg VA 23185-4147
Tel: 800-616-6164
http://www.ncsconline.org

This is the oldest and largest professional association for prosecutors in the world.

National District Attorneys Association
44 Canal Center Plaza, Suite 110
Alexandria, VA 22314-1548
Tel: 703-549-9222
http://www.ndaa.org

For information on judicial education, contact
National Judicial College
University of Nevada-Reno
Judicial College Building, MS 358
Reno, NV 89557-0001
Tel: 800-255-8343
http://www.judges.org

This professional organization for law faculty and law school administrators seeks "to make the legal profession more inclusive, to enhance the quality of legal education, and to extend the power of legal representation to under-served individuals and communities." Visit its Web site for more information on earnings for law professors.

Society of American Law Teachers
Touro Law Center
Public Advocacy Center, Room 223
225 Eastview Drive
Central Islip, NY 11722-4539
Tel: 631-650-2310
http://www.saltlaw.org

For information on the Supreme Court, such as recent rulings, contact
Supreme Court of the United States
One First Street, NE
Washington, DC 20543-0001
Tel: 202-479-3000
http://www.supremecourt.gov

Lobbyists

OVERVIEW

A *lobbyist* works to influence legislation on the federal, state, or local level on behalf of clients. Nonprofit organizations, labor unions, trade associations, corporations, and other groups and individuals use lobbyists to voice concerns and opinions to government representatives. Lobbyists use their knowledge of the legislative process and their government contacts to represent their clients' interests. Though most lobbyists are based in Washington, D.C., many work throughout the country representing client issues in city and state government.

HISTORY

Lobbying has been a practice within government since colonial times. In the late 1700s, the term *lobbyist* was used to describe the special-interest representatives who gathered in the anteroom outside the legislative chamber in the New York state capitol. The term often had a negative connotation, with political cartoonists frequently portraying lobbyists as slick, cigar-chomping individuals attempting to buy favors. But in the 20th century, lobbyists came to be looked upon as experts in the fields that they represented, and members of Congress relied upon them to provide information needed to evaluate legislation. During the New Deal in the 1930s, government spending in Washington greatly increased, and the number of lobbyists proliferated proportionately. A major lobbying law was enacted in 1938, but it was not until 1946 that comprehensive legislation in the form of the Federal Regulation of Lobbying Act was passed into law. The act requires that anyone

QUICK FACTS

School Subjects
Government
Journalism
Speech

Personal Skills
Communication/ideas
Leadership/management

Work Environment
Primarily indoors
One location with some travel

Minimum Education Level
Bachelor's degree

Salary Range
$20,000 to $113,327 to $500,000+

Certification or Licensing
None available

Outlook
About as fast as the average

DOT
165

GOE
N/A

NOC
N/A

O*NET-SOC
N/A

who spends or receives money or anything of value in the interests of passing, modifying, or defeating legislation being considered by the U.S. Congress be registered and provide spending reports. Its effectiveness, however, was reduced by vague language that frequently required legal interpretations. Further regulatory acts have been passed in the years since; most recently, the Lobbying Disclosure Act of 1995 has required registration of all lobbyists working at the federal level.

THE JOB

An example of effective lobbying concerns MedicAlert, an organization that provides bracelets to millions of people in the United States and Canada with health problems. Engraved on the bracelet is a description of the person's medical problem, along with MedicAlert's 24-hour emergency response phone number. The emergency response center is located in a region of California that considered changing the telephone area code. MedicAlert anticipated a lot of confusion—and many possible medical disasters—if the area code was changed from that which is engraved on the millions of bracelets. MedicAlert called upon doctors, nurses, and the media to get word out about the danger to lives. Through this lobbying, the public and the state's policy makers became aware of an important aspect of the area code change they may not have otherwise known.

The MedicAlert Foundation, like the thousands of associations, unions, and corporations in the United States, benefited from using lobbyists with an understanding of state politics and influence. The ASAE/Center for Association Leadership estimates that the number of national trade and charitable associations is over 20,000. With 3,500 of these associations based in Washington, D.C., associations are the third-largest industry in the city, behind government and tourism. Lobbyists may work for one of these associations as a director of government relations, or they may work for an industry, company, or other organization to act on its behalf in government concerns. Lobbyists also work for lobbying firms that work with many different clients on a contractual basis.

Lobbyists have years of experience working with the government, learning about federal and state politics, and meeting career politicians and their staffs. Their job is to make members of Congress aware of the issues of concern to their clients and the effect that legislation and regulations will have on them. They provide the members of Congress with research and analysis to help them make the most informed decisions possible. Lobbyists also keep their clients informed with updates and reports.

Tom McNamara is the president of a government relations firm based in Washington, D.C. He first became involved in politics by working on campaigns before he was even old enough to vote. Throughout his years in government work, he has served as the chief of staff for two different members of Congress and was active in both the Reagan and Bush presidential campaigns. "Clients hire me for my advice," McNamara says. "They ask me to do strategic planning, relying on my knowledge of how Congress operates." After learning about a client's problem, McNamara researches the issue, then develops a plan and a proposal to solve the problem. Some of the questions he must ask when seeking a solution are: What are our assets? Who can we talk to who has the necessary influence? Do we need the media? Do we need to talk to congressional staff members? "With 22 years in the House of Representatives," McNamara says, "I have a tremendous base of people I know. Part of my work is maintaining these relationships, as well as developing relationships with new members and their staff."

Lobbying techniques are generally broken down into two broad categories: direct lobbying and indirect, or "grassroots," lobbying. Direct lobbying techniques include making personal contacts with members of Congress and appointed officials. It is important for lobbyists to know who the key people are in drafting legislation that is significant to their clientele. They hire technical experts to develop reports, charts, graphs, or schematic drawings that may help in the legislative decision-making process that determines the passage, amendment, or defeat of a measure. Sometimes a lobbyist with expertise on a particular issue works directly with a member of Congress in the drafting of a bill. Lobbyists also keep members of Congress tuned in to the voices of their constituents.

Indirect, or grassroots, lobbying involves persuading voters to support a client's view. If the Congress member knows that a majority of voters favor a particular point of view, he or she will support or fight legislation according to the voters' wishes. Probably the most widely used method of indirect lobbying is the letter-writing campaign. Lobbyists use direct mail, newsletters, e-mails, social networking Web sites, blogs, microblogs, media advertising, and other methods of communication to reach the constituents and convince them to contact their member of Congress with their supporting views. Lobbyists also use phone campaigns, encouraging the constituents to call their Congress member's office. Aides usually tally the calls that come in and communicate the volume to the legislator.

Politics on the Web

CNN Politics
http://www.cnn.com/POLITICS

C-SPAN.org
http://www.cspan.org

The Hill
http://thehill.com

Kids Voting USA
http://www.kidsvotingusa.org

The *New York Times*: Politics
http://www.nytimes.com/pages/politics

Rock the Vote
http://www.rockthevote.com

Roll Call
http://www.rollcall.com

U.S. House of Representatives
http://www.house.gov

U.S. Senate
http://www.senate.gov

The White House
http://www.whitehouse.gov

Indirect lobbying is also done through the media. Lobbyists try to persuade newspaper and magazine editors and radio and television news managers to write or air editorials that reflect the point of view of their clientele. They write op-ed pieces that are submitted to the media for publication. They arrange for experts to speak in favor of a particular position on talk shows or to make statements that are picked up by the media. As a persuasive measure, lobbyists may send a legislator a collection of news clippings indicating public opinion on a forthcoming measure, or provide recordings of aired editorials and news features covering a relevant subject.

REQUIREMENTS

High School
Becoming a lobbyist requires years of experience in other government and related positions. To prepare for a government job, take

courses in history, social studies, and civics to learn about the structure of local, state, and federal government. English and composition classes will help you develop your communication skills. Work on the student council or become an officer for a school club. Taking journalism courses and working on the school newspaper will prepare you for the public relations aspect of lobbying. As a reporter you will research current issues, meet with policy makers, and write articles.

Postsecondary Training

As a rule, people take up lobbying after having left an earlier career. As mentioned earlier, Tom McNamara worked for over 20 years as a congressional staff member before moving on to this other aspect of government work. (See the article Congressional Aides for more information about working for a member of Congress.) Schools do not generally offer a specific curriculum that leads to a career as a lobbyist; your experience with legislation and policy making is what will prove valuable to employers and clients. Almost all lobbyists have college degrees, and many have graduate degrees. Degrees in law and political science are among the most beneficial for prospective lobbyists, just as they are for other careers in politics and government. Journalism, education, public relations, history, and economics are other areas of study that would be helpful in the pursuit of a lobbying career.

The American League of Lobbyists (ALL) offers a certificate program for newcomers to the field, as well as experienced practitioners who wish to brush up on their skills. To complete the ALL Lobbying Certificate Program, applicants must take 11 of the following 14 sessions: Lobbying 101; Online Advocacy; Political Action Committees and Campaign Finance (required); Ethics in Lobbying (required); State Lobbying; Grassroots & Coalitions; Lobbying Disclosure & Compliance (required); Budget & Appropriations; Congressional Rules & Procedures (required); Legislative Drafting; Executive Branch Lobbying; Communications & Media (required); Federal Contracting & Regulatory Affairs; and The Business of Lobbying.

Certification or Licensing

Lobbyists do not need a license or certification, but are required to register. The Lobbying Disclosure Act of 1995 requires all lobbyists working on the federal level to register with the Secretary of the Senate and the Clerk of the House. You may also be required to register with the states in which you lobby and possibly pay a small fee.

There is no union available to lobbyists. Some lobbyists join the American League of Lobbyists, which provides a variety of support services for its members. Membership in a number of other associations, including the ASAE/Center for Association Leadership and the American Association of Political Consultants, can also be useful to lobbyists.

Other Requirements

"I've had practical, everyday involvement in government and politics," McNamara says about the skills and knowledge most valuable to him as a lobbyist. "I know what motivates Congress members and staff to act."

In addition to this understanding, McNamara emphasizes that lobbyists must be honest in all their professional dealings with others. "The only way to be successful is to be completely honest and straightforward." Your career will be based on your reputation as a reliable person, so you must be very scrupulous in building that reputation.

You also need people skills to develop good relationships with legislators in order to serve your clients' interests. Your knowledge of the workings of government, along with good communication skills, will help you to explain government legislation to your clients in ways that they can clearly understand.

EXPLORING

To explore this career, become an intern or volunteer in the office of a lobbyist, legislator, government official, special interest group, or nonprofit institution (especially one that relies on government grants). Working in these fields will introduce you to the lobbyist's world and provide early exposure to the workings of government.

Another good way to learn more about this line of work is by becoming involved in your school government; writing for your school newspaper; doing public relations, publicity, and advertising work for school and community organizations; and taking part in fund-raising drives. When major legislative issues are being hotly debated, you can contact your congressional representatives to express your views or even organize a letter-writing or telephone campaign; these actions are in themselves forms of lobbying.

EMPLOYERS

Organizations either hire government liaisons to handle lobbying or they contract with law and lobby firms. Liaisons who work for one organization work on only those issues that affect that organization.

Independent lobbyists work on a variety of different issues, taking on clients on a contractual basis. They may contract with large corporations, such as a pharmaceutical or communications company, as well as volunteer services to nonprofit organizations. Lobbying firms are located all across the country. Those executives in charge of government relations for trade associations and other organizations are generally based in Washington, D.C.

STARTING OUT

Lobbyist positions will not be listed in the classifieds. It takes years of experience and an impressive list of connections to find a government relations job in an organization. Tom McNamara retired at age 50 from his work with the House of Representatives. "Lobbying was a natural progression into the private sector," he says. His love for public policy, campaigns, and politics led him to start his own lobbying firm. "I had an institutional understanding that made me valuable," he says.

Professional lobbyists usually have backgrounds as lawyers, public relations executives, congressional aides, legislators, government officials, or professionals in business and industry. Once established in a government or law career, lobbyists begin to hear about corporations, nonprofit organizations, and associations that need knowledgeable people for their government relations departments. The ASAE & Center for Association Leadership's Web site, http://www.asaecenter.org, lists available positions for executives with trade associations.

ADVANCEMENT

Lobbyists focus on developing long-standing relationships with legislators and clients and becoming experts on policy making and legislation. Association or company executives may advance from a position as director of government relations into a position as president or vice president. Lobbyists who contract their services to various clients advance by taking on more clients and working for larger corporations.

EARNINGS

Because of the wide range of salaries earned by lobbyists, it is difficult to compile an accurate survey. According to Salary.com, government affairs directors (a career field that includes lobbyists) earned median annual salaries of $113,327 in 2010. Salaries ranged from less than $72,245, while the most experienced workers earned more than $154,457.

Like lawyers, lobbyists are considered very well paid; also like lawyers, a lobbyist's income depends on the size of the organization he or she represents. Experienced contract lobbyists with a solid client base can earn well over $100,000 a year and some make more than $500,000 a year. Beginning lobbyists may make less than $20,000 a year as they build a client base. In many cases, a lobbyist may take on large corporations as clients for the bulk of the annual income, then volunteer services to nonprofit organizations.

WORK ENVIRONMENT

Lobbyists spend much of their time communicating with the people who affect legislation—principally the legislators and officials of federal and state governments. This communication takes place in person, by telephone, by e-mail, and by memoranda. Most of a lobbyist's time is spent gathering information, writing reports, creating publicity, and staying in touch with clients. They respond to the public and the news media when required. Sometimes their expertise is required at hearings or they may testify before a legislature.

Tom McNamara has enjoyed the change from congressional chief of staff to lobbyist. "I'm an integral part of the system of government," he says, "albeit in a different role." He feels that every day is distinctly different, and he has the opportunity to meet new and interesting people. "It's intellectually challenging," he says. "You have to stay on top of the issues, and keep track of the personalities as well as the campaigns."

OUTLOOK

The number of special interest groups in the United States continues to grow, and as long as they continue to plead their causes before state and federal governments, lobbyists will be needed. However, lobbying cutbacks often occur in corporations. Because lobbying doesn't directly earn a profit for a business, the government relations department is often the first in a company to receive budget cuts. The American League of Lobbyists anticipates that the career will remain stable, though it's difficult to predict. In recent years, there has been a significant increase in registrations, but that is most likely a result of the Lobbying Disclosure Act of 1995 requiring registration.

The methods of grassroots advocacy will continue to be affected by the Internet and other new communication technology. Lobbyists and organizations use Web pages to inform the public of policy issues. These Web pages often include ways to immediately send e-mail messages to state and federal legislators. Constituents may have the choice of composing their own messages or sending messages already composed. With this method, a member of Congress can easily determine the feelings of the constituents based on the amount of e-mail received.

FOR MORE INFORMATION

For information on membership, contact
American Association of Political Consultants
8400 Westpark Drive, 2nd Floor
McLean, VA 22102-5116
Tel: 703-245-8020
http://www.theaapc.org

For information about careers and its Lobbying Certificate Program, contact
American League of Lobbyists
PO Box 30005
Alexandria, VA 22310-8005
Tel: 703-960-3011
E-mail: alldc.org@erols.com
http://www.alldc.org

For information about government relations and public policy concerns within trade associations, contact
The ASAE & Center for Association Leadership
1575 I Street, NW
Washington, DC 20005-1105
Tel: 888-950-2723
http://www.asaecenter.org

For resources for women lobbyists, contact
Women in Government Relations
801 North Fairfax Street, Suite 211
Alexandria, VA 22314-1757
Tel: 703-299-8546
http://www.wgr.org

Political Columnists and Writers

QUICK FACTS

School Subjects
English
Government
Journalism

Personal Skills
Communication/ideas
Helping/teaching

Work Environment
Indoors and outdoors
Primarily multiple locations

Minimum Education Level
Bachelor's degree

Salary Range
$19,650 to $34,360 to
$74,700+ (columnists)
$28,070 to $53,900 to
$105,710+ (writers)

Certification or Licensing
None available

Outlook
Decline (columnists)
About as fast as the average
(writers)

DOT
131

GOE
01.03.01 (columnists)
01.02.01 (writers)

NOC
5123 (columnists)
5121 (writers)

O*NET-SOC
27-3022.00 (columnists)
27-3043.00 (writers)

OVERVIEW

Political columnists write opinion pieces about politics and government for publication in newspapers and magazines. Some columnists work for syndicates, which are organizations that sell articles to many media at once.

Political writers express, edit, promote, and interpret ideas and facts about politics and government in written form for newspapers, magazines, books, Web sites, and radio and television broadcasts.

HISTORY

Writers have been reporting and commenting on politics and government ever since newspapers and magazines were first published. The first American newspaper, *Publick Occurrences Both Foreign and Domestick*, appeared in Boston in 1690, but lasted only one issue due to censorship by the British government. The first continuously published newspaper in America was the *Boston News-Letter*, first published in 1704. In 1728, Benjamin Franklin began publishing the *Pennsylvania Gazette*. Known today as *The New York Times*, it has been influential in setting a high standard for American journalists. Franklin also published the first magazine in the colonies, *The American Magazine*, in 1741. The first daily newspaper, the *Pennsylvania Evening Post*, began publication in 1783.

Because the earliest American newspapers were political vehicles, much of their news stories brimmed with commentary and opinion. This practice continued up until the Civil War. Horace Greeley, a popular editor who had regularly espoused partisanship in his *New York Tribune*, was the first to give editorial opinion its own page separate from the news. As newspapers grew into instruments of mass communication, their editors sought balance and fairness on the editorial pages and began publishing a number of columns with varying viewpoints. Today, political columnists and writers such as Art Buchwald and Molly Ivins were well known for their satirical look at government and politicians. George Will, Kathleen Parker, and Fareed Zakaria are known for their keen analysis and opinions about government and world events.

The invention of radio and television in the 20th century and the growth of news and commentary on the Internet have only added to the power of political columnists and writers as their thoughts, ideas, and opinions are read and heard by millions or even billions throughout the world.

THE JOB

Political columnists often take news stories about politics or government and enhance the facts with personal opinions and panache. Political columnists may also write from their personal experiences. Either way, a column usually has a punchy start, a pithy middle, and a strong, sometimes poignant, ending.

Political columnists are responsible for writing columns on a regular basis on accord with a schedule, depending on the frequency of publication. They may write a column daily, weekly, monthly, or quarterly. Others may write a blog or microblog on Twitter in addition to writing a standard column. Like other journalists, they face pressure to meet a deadline.

Most political columnists are free to select their own story ideas. The need to constantly come up with new and interesting ideas may be one of the hardest parts of the job, but also one of the most rewarding. Columnists search through newspapers, magazines, and the Internet, watch television, and listen to the radio. The various types of media suggest ideas and keep the writer aware of current events and social issues. Political columnists also attend political rallies, legislative sessions, press conferences, and other events to gather information and find column ideas.

Next, they do research, delving into a topic—such as government corruption, attempts by a state legislature to pass an annual budget, or a senator's stance on a controversial issue—much like an investigative reporter would, so that they can back up their arguments with facts.

Finally, they write, usually on a computer. After a column is written, at least one editor goes over it to check for clarity and correct mistakes. Then the cycle begins again.

Staff writers who specialize in political writing are employed by magazines and newspapers to write news stories, feature articles, and columns about politics; government; local, regional, or national news; and any other topic (education, health, consumer affairs, etc.) that may occasionally fall under the political spectrum. First they come up with an idea for an article from their own interests or are assigned a topic by an editor. The topic is of relevance to the particular publication; for example, a writer for a magazine that specializes in national politics may be assigned an article on the presidential election. Another writer may be assigned an article about a political scandal, the rise of a political family (like the Kennedys or the Bushes) and their role in government today, the emergence of a new political movement such as the Tea Party, or a senatorial race that is being contested on the basis of alleged election fraud. Then writers begin gathering as much information as possible about the subject through library research, interviews, the Internet, observation, and other methods. They keep extensive notes from which they will draw material for their project. Once the material has been organized and arranged in logical sequence, writers prepare a written outline. The process of developing a piece of writing is exciting, although it can also involve detailed and solitary work. After researching an idea, a writer might discover that a different perspective or related topic would be more effective, entertaining, or marketable.

Political editorial writers write about political or government-related topics for newspapers, magazines, and Web sites (including blogs). Their comments, consistent with the viewpoints and policies of their employers, are intended to stimulate or mold public opinion.

Writers can also work as *political reporters*, who gather and analyze information about political-related topics and write stories for publication or for broadcasting.

Newswriters who specialize in political writing work for radio and TV news departments and news-oriented Web sites. They write politically focused news stories, news "teases," special features, and investigative reports by researching and fact checking information obtained from reporters, news wires, press releases, research, and telephone and e-mail interviews. Newswriters must be able to write clear, concise

José Díaz-Balart, anchor of Telemundo's *Enfoque* (*left*), and Ron Brownstein, a columnist for the *National Journal*, appear on *Meet the Press*, a weekly television news show. *(William B. Plowman, NBC NewsWire via AP Images)*

stories that fit in an allotted time period. Newswriters employed in television broadcasting must be able to match the words they write with the images that are broadcast to help illustrate the story. Since most radio and television stations broadcast 24 hours a day, newswriters are needed to work daytime, evening, and overnight shifts.

When working on assignment, all political writers submit their outlines to an editor or other company representative for approval. Then they write a first draft, trying to put the material into words that will have the desired effect on their audience. They often rewrite or polish sections of the material as they proceed, always searching for just the right way of imparting information or expressing an idea or opinion. A manuscript may be reviewed, corrected, and revised numerous times before a final copy is submitted. Even after that, an editor may request additional changes.

Political writers can be employed either as in-house staff or as freelancers. Pay varies according to experience and the position, but freelancers must provide their own office space and equipment such as computers and fax machines. Freelancers also must keep tax records, send out invoices, search for new work, negotiate contracts, and provide their own health insurance.

REQUIREMENTS

High School

Most newspapers and magazines expect their political columnists and writers to have a college education, so you will need to graduate from high school to be accepted into a college or university. As a high school student, you should take as many writing and English classes as you can. You should also take classes in current events, political science, history, and government. Also, learn as much about computers as you can. Finally, taking a typing or keyboarding class is a good idea.

Postsecondary Training

As is the case for other journalists, at least a bachelor's degree in journalism is usually required to become a political columnist or writer, although some journalists graduate with degrees in political science or English. Visit the Web site of the Accrediting Council on Education in Journalism and Mass Communications (http://www2.ku.edu/~acejmc/STUDENT/PROGLIST.SHTML) for a list of accredited postsecondary training programs in journalism and mass communications. You can gain experience by writing for your college or university newspaper and through a summer internship at a newspaper or other publication. It also may be helpful to submit freelance opinion columns to local or national publications that feature content that is of a political nature. The more published articles (called clips) you can show to prospective employers, the better.

Other Requirements

Political columnists and writers need to be curious, have a genuine interest in people, the ability to write clearly and succinctly, and the strength to thrive under deadline pressure. Political columnists also require a certain wit and wisdom, the compunction to express strong opinions, and the ability to take apart an issue and debate it.

EXPLORING

A good way to explore this career is to work for your school newspaper and perhaps write your own column or feature stories. Participation in debate clubs will help you form opinions and express them clearly. Read your city's newspaper regularly, and take a look at national papers as well as magazines. Which political columnists or writers, on the local and national level, interest you? Why do you feel their columns or articles are well done? Try to incorporate these good qualities into your own writing. Contact your local newspaper and ask for a tour of the facilities. This will give you a sense of what the office atmosphere is like and what technologies are used there. Ask to speak with one of the paper's regular political columnists or writers about his or her job. He or she may be able to provide you with valuable insights. Visit the Dow Jones Newspaper Fund Web site (https://www.newsfund.org) for information on careers, summer programs, internships, and more. Try getting a part-time or summer job at a newspaper, even if it's just answering phones and doing data entry. In this way you'll be able to test out how well you like working in such an atmosphere.

EMPLOYERS

Newspapers of all kinds run political columns and articles, as do certain magazines and even public radio stations, where a recording is played over the airways of the author reading the column or article. Newswriters are employed by radio and television stations throughout the country, although more opportunities are available in larger media markets. Many political columnists and writers work for mainstream news organizations that have a presence on the Internet, as well as new media outlets that exist solely on the Internet. Some political columnists and writers are self-employed, preferring to market their work to syndicates instead of working for a single newspaper or magazine. Some political columnists and writers have their own Web sites.

STARTING OUT

Political columnists and writers break into the field by working in entry-level journalism jobs such as fact checker, research assistant, or editorial assistant. With experience, they can eventually find positions as political writers or reporters. Political writers and reporters who demonstrate comprehensive knowledge of politics and government, and who demonstrate a knack for lively, opinionated writing, may be offered the position of political columnist.

Another way to become a political columnist or writer is to start out by freelancing, sending columns or articles out to a multitude of newspapers and magazines in the hopes that someone will pick them up. Also, columnists and writers can market their work to syndicates. A list of these, and magazines that may also be interested

in political writing, is provided in the *Writer's Market* (http://www
.writersmarket.com).

ADVANCEMENT

Political columnists and writers can advance in national exposure
by having their work syndicated. They also may try to get a collection of their columns or articles published in book form. Moving
from a small newspaper or magazine to a large national publication
is another way to advance for columnists and writers. Newswriters who are employed by radio and television stations can advance
by moving to the same positions at stations in larger—and more
prestigious—markets. Others may choose to become print or broadcast reporters.

Political columnists and writers also may choose to work in other
editorial positions, such as managing editor, editor, page editor, or
foreign correspondent.

EARNINGS

Like reporters' salaries, the incomes of political columnists and writers vary greatly according to experience; newspaper, magazine, radio
station, or television station size and location; and whether the columnist or writer is under a union contract. The U.S. Department
of Labor (DOL) classifies columnists with news analysts, reporters,
and correspondents, and reports that the median annual income for
these professionals was $34,360 in 2009. Ten percent of those in
this group earned less than $19,650, and 10 percent made more than
$74,700 annually. Popular columnists at large papers earn consider-
ably higher salaries.

In 2009, median earnings for all salaried writers were $53,900 a
year, according to the DOL. The lowest paid 10 percent earned less
than $28,070, while the highest paid 10 percent earned $105,710
or more. Writers employed by newspaper and book publishers had
annual mean earnings of $53,050, while those employed in radio
and television broadcasting earned $65,330.

Freelancers may be paid by the column or article. Syndicates pay
columnists and other writers 40 percent to 60 percent of the sales
income generated by their columns or articles, or a flat fee if only
one column or article is being sold.

Freelancers must provide their own benefits. Political columnists
and writers working on staff at newspapers and magazines receive

typical benefits such as health insurance, paid vacation days, sick days, and retirement plans.

WORK ENVIRONMENT

Most political columnists and writers work in newsrooms or offices. The atmosphere in a newsroom is generally fast paced and loud, so political columnists and writers must be able to concentrate and meet deadlines in this type of environment. Some political writers—especially those who are syndicated but not affiliated with a particular newspaper, magazine, or Web site—work out of their homes or private offices.

Political columnists and writers occasionally travel to conduct interviews or do research on location. They may travel to government offices, state capitals, courthouses, political demonstrations, political conventions, press conferences, foreign countries, and other settings to gather information for columns and articles. Some political columnists and writers work more than 40 hours a week.

OUTLOOK

The DOL predicts that employment growth for news analysts, reporters, and correspondents (including political columnists) will decline through 2018. The employment of writers (including political writers) is expected to increase about as fast as the average rate of all occupations through 2018, according to the DOL.

Growth will be hindered by such factors as mergers and closures of newspapers, decreasing circulation, and lower profits from advertising revenue. However, online publications will continue to be a source for new jobs. Competition for newspaper and magazine positions is very competitive, and competition for the positions of political columnist and political writer is even stiffer because these are prestigious jobs that are limited in number. It may be easier to find employment at smaller daily and weekly newspapers than at major metropolitan newspapers, and movement up the ladder will also likely be quicker. Pay, however, is lower at smaller newspapers. Journalism and mass communication graduates will have the best opportunities, and writers will be needed to replace those who leave the field for other work or retire.

Employment for all positions in the radio and television broadcasting industry is expected to increase about 7 percent, more slowly than the average for all industries through 2018, according to the DOL.

FOR MORE INFORMATION

The ACEJMC is "responsible for the evaluation of professional journalism and mass communications programs in colleges and universities." Visit its Web site for a list of accredited programs.
Accrediting Council on Education in Journalism and Mass Communications (ACEJMC)
University of Kansas School of Journalism and Mass Communications
Stauffer-Flint Hall
1435 Jayhawk Boulevard
Lawrence, KS 66045-7575
Tel: 785-864-3973
http://www2.ku.edu/~acejmc

The society provides information on careers in reporting, as well as details on education and financial aid (from outside sources).
American Society of Journalists and Authors
1501 Broadway, Suite 403
New York, NY 10036-5507
Tel: 212-997-0947
http://www.asja.org

This organization provides general educational information on all areas of journalism, including newspapers, magazines, television, Internet, and radio. Members include journalism and mass communication faculty, administrators, students, and media professionals.
Association for Education in Journalism and Mass Communication
234 Outlet Pointe Boulevard
Columbia, SC 29210-5667
Tel: 803-798-0271
E-mail: aejmchq@aol.com
http://www.aejmc.org

An association of university broadcasting faculty, industry professionals, and graduate students, BEA offers annual scholarships in broadcasting for college juniors, seniors, and graduate students. Visit its Web site for useful information about broadcast education and the broadcasting industry.
Broadcast Education Association
1771 N Street, NW
Washington, DC 20036-2891

Tel: 202-429-3935
http://www.beaweb.org

*Visit the fund's Web site for information on print and online jour-
nalism careers, college and university journalism programs, high
school journalism workshops, scholarships, internships, and job
listings.*
   Dow Jones Newspaper Fund
   PO Box 300
   Princeton, NJ 08543-0300
   Tel: 609-452-2820
   E-mail: djnf@dowjones.com
   https://www.newsfund.org

*The EFA is an organization for freelance editors, writers, and other
publishing professionals. Members receive a newsletter and a free
listing in its directory.*
   Editorial Freelancers Association (EFA)
   71 West 23rd Street, 4th Floor
   New York, NY 10010-4102
   Tel: 212-929-5400
   E-mail: office@the-efa.org
   http://www.the-efa.org

*The association provides information on broadcast education,
scholarships for college students, jobs, and useful publications at
its Web site.*
   National Association of Broadcasters
   1771 N Street, NW
   Washington, DC 20036-2800
   Tel: 202-429-5300
   E-mail: nab@nab.org
   http://www.nab.org

*Visit the conference's Web site for information on membership and
scholarships for college students and answers to frequently asked
questions about a career as an editorial writer.*
   National Conference of Editorial Writers
   3899 North Front Street
   Harrisburg, PA 17110-1583
   Tel: 717-703-3015
   E-mail: ncew@pa-news.org
   http://www.ncew.org

This nonprofit trade association represents the owners, publishers, and editors of community newspapers in the United States.
National Newspaper Association
PO Box 7540
Columbia, MO 65205-7540
Tel: 573-882-5800
http://www.nnaweb.org

Visit the society's Web site for information on membership and scholarships for college students and to read The Columnist *newsletter.*
National Society of Newspaper Columnists
PO Box 411532
San Francisco, CA 94141-1532
Tel: 415-488-6762
http://www.columnists.com

This is a trade union for "freelance and contract writers: journalists, book authors, business and technical writers, web content providers, and poets." Visit its Web site for resources for journalists and writers.
National Writers Union
256 West 38th Street, Suite 703
New York, NY 10018-9807
Tel: 212-254-0279
E-mail: nwu@nwu.org
http://www.nwu.org

This nonprofit organization represents the $47 billion newspaper industry and more than 2,000 newspapers in the United States and Canada. Visit its Web site for information on trends in the industry and careers (including digital media job descriptions).
Newspaper Association of America
4401 Wilson Boulevard, Suite 900
Arlington, VA 22203-1867
Tel: 571-366-1000
http://www.naa.org

The guild is a union for journalists, advertising sales workers, and other media professionals.
The Newspaper Guild-Communication Workers of America
501 Third Street, NW, 6th Floor
Washington, DC 20001-2797

Tel: 202-434-7177
E-mail: guild@cwa-union.org
http://www.newsguild.org

The Online News Association is a membership organization for journalists "whose principal livelihood involves gathering or producing news for digital presentation." Members include "news writers, producers, designers, editors, photographers, technologists and others who produce news for the Internet or other digital delivery systems, as well as academic members and others interested in the development of online." Visit its Web site for information on membership for high school and college students.
Online News Association
E-mail: director@journalists.org
http://journalists.org

Visit this organization's Web site to access scholarship and internship information (for college students), high school journalism resources and programs (such as the High School Broadcast Journalism Project), useful publications, and salary and employment surveys. The association also offers membership to college students.
Radio Television Digital News Association
529 14th Street, NW, Suite 425
Washington, DC 20045-1406
Tel: 202-659-6510
http://www.rtdna.org

Visit the society's Web site for information on student chapters and scholarships for college students, job listings, training opportunities, educational resources, discussion boards and blogs, and much more.
Society of Professional Journalists
3909 North Meridian Street
Indianapolis, IN 46208-4011
Tel: 317-927-8000
http://www.spj.org

Visit the following Web site for comprehensive information on journalism careers, summer programs, and college journalism programs:
High School Journalism
http://www.hsj.org

Political Reporters

QUICK FACTS

School Subjects
English
Government
Journalism
Speech

Personal Skills
Communication/ideas
Helping/teaching

Work Environment
Indoors and outdoors
Primarily multiple locations

Minimum Education Level
Bachelor's degree

Salary Range
$19,650 to $51,570 to
$74,700+

Certification or Licensing
None available

Outlook
Decline

DOT
131

GOE
01.03.01

NOC
5123

O*NET-SOC
27-3021.00, 27-3022.00

OVERVIEW

Political reporters gather and analyze information about current events in government and politics and broadcast their reports on radio and television stations. Political reporters are also employed by newspapers and magazines. For more information on careers in print journalism, see Political Columnists and Writers. Radio and television reporters, news analysts, and correspondents hold approximately 9,850 jobs in the United States.

HISTORY

Instantaneous worldwide communication first became a reality in 1895 when an Italian engineer named Guglielmo Marconi demonstrated how to send communication signals without the use of wires. In the early 1900s, transmitting and receiving devices were relatively simple, and hundreds of amateurs constructed transmitters and receivers on their own and experimented with radio. In 1906, Reginald A. Fessenden achieved two-way human voice transmission via radio between Massachusetts and Scotland. Small radio shows started in 1910; in 1920, two commercial radio stations went on the air; and by 1921, a dozen local stations were broadcasting. By 1926, stations across the country were linked together to form the National Broadcasting Company (NBC). Four years later, the first radio broadcast was made around the world. Radio, along with newspapers and magazines, served as the primary source of news for Americans in the pre-television era.

Modern television developed from experiments with electricity and vacuum tubes in the mid-1800s, but it was not until 1939, when

President Franklin D. Roosevelt used television to open the New York World's Fair, that the public realized the power of television as a means of communication. Several stations went on the air shortly after this demonstration and successfully televised sporting events and the Republican and Democratic conventions of 1940. The onset of World War II limited the further development of television until after the war was over.

Since television's strength is the immediacy with which it can present information, news programs became the foundation of regular programming. *Meet the Press* premiered in 1947, followed by nightly newscasts in 1948. In the 1950s, the Federal Communications Commission lifted a freeze on the processing of station applications, and the number of commercial stations grew steadily, from 120 in 1953 to more than 2,200 broadcasting television stations today.

It was in the 1960s that television's power became most apparent: together the country mourned the death of President John F. Kennedy; witnessed the murder of his alleged assassin, Lee Harvey Oswald, by Jack Ruby, and formed opinions on the Vietnam War based on live TV news footage and commentary from political reporters.

In the following decades, political reporters continued to play a pivotal role in educating the public about important news events, including Watergate, the attempted assassination of President Ronald Reagan, the Persian Gulf War, the impeachment hearings of President Clinton, the contested presidential election of 2000, the government's response to the terrorist attacks of September 11, 2001, and countless other political issues of local, regional, national, or international importance.

THE JOB

Political reporters collect information on newsworthy events of a political nature and prepare stories for radio or television broadcast. Typical stories that a political reporter might cover include an election campaign (e.g., candidate debates, rallies, conventions, and speeches); a debate between Democratic and Republican state legislators over a controversial gun control bill; a rally by the Tea Party that advocates for a reduction of the federal deficit; a ghost payroll scandal at top levels of government; the controversial closing of state-run hospitals by elected officials; an antiwar demonstration on the steps of Capitol Hill; and a president's speech to the United Nations urging sanctions against a country that is purported to be developing weapons of mass destruction.

Political reporters may present stories that simply provide information about local, state, national, or international events, or they may present opposing points of view on issues of current political interest. In this latter capacity, the press plays an important role in monitoring the actions of public officials and others in positions of power.

Political reporters may receive story assignments from an editor, producer, or news director, or as the result of a lead, or news tip. Good political reporters are always on the lookout for story ideas.

To cover a story, political reporters gather and verify facts by interviewing people involved in or related to the event, examining documents and public records, observing events as they happen, and researching relevant background information. Political reporters generally take notes, use an audio recording device, or shoot footage using a video camera as they collect information. TV reporters may shoot the footage themselves or bring a camera operator to the scene. Radio reporters typically work alone on the news scene, though they may be assisted by engineers. It is important for radio and TV reporters to understand the latest video and audio equipment.

After taping an interview, the political reporter will then review the material and determine which information is most significant to the story, as well as edit the material and incorporate any other information he or she has obtained, according to the time allotted for the report. The TV political reporter looks for the most interesting quotes from the interview subject, and the most relevant visuals and sounds. Often, political reporters go live at the scene of a news event; the reporter will then introduce the news segment during the newscast and answer questions from the anchor about the story. Political reporters who work for traditional radio stations don't have video to help them tell the story. They must rely on audio and their ability to paint a vivid picture of the newsworthy events. Radio stations that have a presence on the Internet often require their reporters to shoot video or photographs of news events that can be posted online.

Political reporters may have specific areas, or "beats," to cover, such as a presidential campaign, city hall, or the state legislature. Most reporters only report on that day's news, but, in some cases, a reporter may spend several days with a particular news story, such as on a news magazine program. An investigative report might also be broadcast as a series within a daily newscast.

Political reporters in small radio or television markets may be required to cover other aspects of the news in their communities. They may also take photographs and help with general office work. Television political reporters may have to be photogenic as well as talented and resourceful; they may at times present live reports, filmed by a mobile camera unit at the scene where the news originates, or

Reporters question U.S. Representative John Boehner (*center*) on the status of legislative negotiations after a meeting of House Republicans on Capitol Hill in Washington, D.C. *(Lauren Victoria Burke, AP Photo)*

they may record interviews and narration for later broadcast. Personal appearance is also important to radio reporters who are filmed for stories that are posted on the Internet.

Many broadcast companies, large newspapers, and magazines have one correspondent who is responsible for covering all the news for the foreign city or country where they are based. These reporters are known as *foreign correspondents*. They report the news by satellite, pre-recorded videotape, telephone, fax, or computer.

Some reporters may work as *commentators*, who interpret specific events and discuss how these may affect individuals or the nation. They may have a specified daily slot for which material must be written, recorded, or presented live. They gather information that is analyzed and interpreted through research and interviews and cover public functions such as political conventions, press conferences, and social events. They also may offer commentary on social or cultural issues. In these instances, their commentary is based more on opinion than on fact.

REQUIREMENTS
High School
High school courses that will provide you with a firm foundation for a political reporting career include English, journalism, political

science, government, history, social studies, communications, typing, and computer science. Speech courses will help you hone your interviewing skills, which are necessary for success as a reporter. In addition, it will be helpful to take college prep courses, such as foreign language, math, and science. Working for your high school newspaper or radio station will provide you with valuable experience interviewing, editing, and writing. Also, become familiar with video and recording equipment by working for your high school's media department.

Postsecondary Training

You will need at least a bachelor's degree to become a political reporter, and a graduate degree will give you a great advantage over those entering the field with lesser degrees. Most editors prefer applicants with degrees in broadcast journalism because their studies include liberal arts courses as well as professional training in journalism. Some editors consider it sufficient for a reporter to have a good general education from a liberal arts college. Others prefer applicants with an undergraduate degree in liberal arts and a master's degree in journalism.

More than 1,500 colleges offer programs in journalism, communications, or related fields. In these schools, around three-fourths of a student's time is devoted to a liberal arts education and one-fourth to the professional study of journalism, with required courses such as introductory mass media, basic reporting and copyediting, history of journalism, and press law and ethics. Students are encouraged to select other journalism courses according to their specific interests. Visit the Web site of the Accrediting Council on Education in Journalism and Mass Communications (http://www2.ku.edu/~acejmc/STUDENT/PROGLIST.SHTML) for a list of accredited postsecondary training programs in journalism and mass communications.

Journalism courses and programs are also offered by many community and junior colleges. Graduates of these programs are prepared to go to work directly as general assignment reporters, but they may encounter difficulty when competing with graduates of four-year programs. Credit earned in community and junior colleges may be transferable to four-year programs in journalism at other colleges and universities. Journalism training may also be obtained in the armed forces. Approximately 200 colleges offer programs in broadcast journalism leading to a bachelor's degree. Broadcast programs require students to take courses like reporting, photography, ethics, and broadcast history. Many schools also have TV and radio stations that either employ students or offer students credit for their work.

Master's degree and Ph.D. programs are also available. Graduate degrees may prepare students specifically for careers in news or as journalism teachers, researchers, and theorists, or for jobs in advertising or public relations. A reporter's liberal arts training should include courses in English (with an emphasis on writing), political science, sociology, economics, history, psychology, business, speech, and computer science. Knowledge of foreign languages is also useful.

Other Requirements
In order to succeed as a political reporter, you must be inquisitive, aggressive, persistent, and detail oriented. You should enjoy interaction with people of various races, cultures, religions, economic levels, and social statuses. You should have a strong interest in the political process and the complexities of government.

EXPLORING

You can explore a career as a political reporter in a number of ways. Working on school radio or television stations and newspapers will provide you with experience as a reporter. You can also try to find part-time work or internships with smaller radio and TV stations or newspapers, which will allow you to observe political reporters and other journalism professionals at work. Finally, contact a local political reporter and ask to spend a few days shadowing him or her to get a sense of the work involved.

EMPLOYERS

Approximately 9,850 radio and television reporters, news analysts, and correspondents are employed at radio and television stations throughout the United States. Newspapers, magazines, book publishers, wire services, and Web sites also employ political reporters.

Four major television networks (ABC, CBS, NBC, and FOX) offer daily news coverage of events of national interest; there are also cable channels (such as CNN, MSNBC, and Fox News) that provide around-the-clock news information. With bureaus in Washington, D.C., New York, London, and other cities, the networks and cable channels provide job opportunities for many political reporters. These positions are highly competitive, however; most broadcast reporters work in cities all across the country for network affiliates, local cable news channels, or radio news stations.

STARTING OUT

Experienced political reporters are in demand throughout the country, although large markets employ the highest number of political reporters. Positions are usually advertised in the local newspapers, or on the job lines of broadcast stations. You may have to submit recordings of your work along with a resume; you should also be persistent in getting your work reviewed for consideration. By doing an online search of broadcasting job listings, you're likely to locate a number of Web sites with descriptions of available positions. You can also find positions in this field through your college's career services office.

ADVANCEMENT

Political reporters may advance by moving to larger radio or television markets, but competition for such positions is unusually keen. Many highly qualified political reporters apply for these jobs every year.

Within a local TV or radio station, a reporter may eventually move on to another area of broadcasting, such as directing or producing a newscast. Reporters also become anchors, who are better paid and more prominent in the newscast. Many more people are employed in sales, promotion, and planning than are employed in reporting and anchoring.

A select number of political reporters eventually become columnists, correspondents, editorial writers, authors, editors, or top executives. These important and influential positions represent the top of the field, and competition for them is strong.

EARNINGS

There are great variations in the earnings of reporters. Salaries are related to experience, the type of employer for which the reporter works, and geographic location. According to the U.S. Department of Labor, the mean salary for reporters and correspondents employed in radio and television was $51,570 in 2009. Salaries for all reporters ranged from less than $19,650 to $74,700 or more annually.

Benefits for full-time workers include vacation and sick time, health, and sometimes dental, insurance, and pension or 401(k) plans. Self-employed reporters must provide their own benefits.

WORK ENVIRONMENT

Political reporters work under a great deal of pressure in settings that differ from the typical business office. Their jobs generally require a five-day, 35- to 40-hour week, but overtime and irregular schedules are very common. Political reporters, especially those who are employed by 24-hour news networks, may work early in the morning or late in the evening to report breaking news stories.

Political reporters work amid the clatter of computer keyboards and other machines, loud voices engaged in telephone conversations, and the bustle created by people hurrying about. An atmosphere of excitement prevails, especially as broadcast deadlines approach.

Travel is often required in this occupation, and some assignments may be dangerous, such as covering wars, political uprisings, demonstrations, and other events of a volatile nature. Other assignments, such as covering a state legislature while it is in session, may require the political reporter to reside in the state's capital for several months at a time.

OUTLOOK

Employment for all types of reporters and correspondents is expected to decline through 2018, according to the *Occupational Outlook Handbook*. Applicants will face strong competition for reporting positions in major broadcast markets. For beginning reporters, stations in smaller markets will provide the best opportunities. Occasionally, a beginner can use contacts and experience gained through internship programs and summer jobs to obtain a reporting job immediately after graduation.

Poor economic conditions do not drastically affect the employment of reporters. Their numbers are not severely cut back even during a downturn; instead, employers forced to reduce expenditures will suspend new hiring.

Technology will continue to have a big impact on the way news is reported. The development of satellite technology and portable high-definition video cameras has revolutionized broadcast journalism over the last 30 years, and new developments over the next 20 years will likely have the same powerful effects. As the Internet competes for TV's viewers and radio's listeners, look for newsrooms to make better use of the technology. Aspiring reporters should learn how to work with audio and video recording technology and digital cameras, and be able to conduct research on the Internet.

FOR MORE INFORMATION

The ACEJMC is "responsible for the evaluation of professional journalism and mass communications programs in colleges and universities." Visit its Web site for a list of accredited programs.

Accrediting Council on Education in Journalism and Mass
   Communications (ACEJMC)
University of Kansas School of Journalism and Mass
   Communications
Stauffer-Flint Hall
1435 Jayhawk Boulevard
Lawrence, KS 66045-7575
Tel: 785-864-3973
http://www2.ku.edu/~acejmc

Contact the alliance for information on careers in radio and television, as well as scholarships and internships for college students.

Alliance for Women in Media
1760 Old Meadow Road, Suite 500
McLean, VA 22102-4306
Tel: 703-506-3290
http://www.awrt.org

The society provides information on careers in reporting, as well as details on education and financial aid (from outside sources).

American Society of Journalists and Authors
1501 Broadway, Suite 403
New York, NY 10036-5507
Tel: 212-997-0947
http://www.asja.org

This organization provides general educational information on all areas of journalism, including newspapers, magazines, television, Internet, and radio. Members include journalism and mass communication faculty, administrators, students, and media professionals.

Association for Education in Journalism and Mass
   Communication
234 Outlet Pointe Boulevard
Columbia, SC 29210-5667
Tel: 803-798-0271
E-mail: aejmchq@aol.com
http://www.aejmc.org

*An association of university broadcasting faculty, industry profes-
sionals, and graduate students, BEA offers annual scholarships in
broadcasting for college juniors, seniors, and graduate students.
Visit its Web site for useful information about broadcast education
and the broadcasting industry.*

Broadcast Education Association
1771 N Street, NW
Washington, DC 20036-2891
Tel: 202-429-3935
http://www.beaweb.org

*For information on investigative journalism and computer-assisted
reporting, contact*

Investigative Reporters and Editors
Missouri School of Journalism
141 Neff Annex
Columbia, MO 65211-0001
Tel: 573-882-2042
E-mail: info@ire.org
http://www.ire.org

*For information on college programs and union membership,
contact*

National Association of Broadcast Employees and Technicians
501 Third Street, NW
Washington, DC 20001-2760
http://www.nabetcwa.org

*The association provides information on broadcast education,
scholarships for college students, jobs, and useful publications at
its Web site.*

National Association of Broadcasters
1771 N Street, NW
Washington, DC 20036-2800
Tel: 202-429-5300
E-mail: nab@nab.org
http://www.nab.org

*The Online News Association is a membership organization for
journalists "whose principal livelihood involves gathering or producing news for digital presentation." Members include "news writers, producers, designers, editors, photographers, technologists and
others who produce news for the Internet or other digital delivery*

systems, as well as academic members and others interested in the development of online." Visit its Web site for information on membership for high school and college students.

Online News Association
E-mail: info@journalists.org
http://www.onlinenewsassociation.org

This professional organization has represented the interests of international journalists since 1939. Visit its Web site for information on scholarships and membership for college students and journalism resources.

Overseas Press Club Foundation
40 West 45 Street
New York, NY 10036-4202
Tel: 212-626-9220
E-mail: info@opcofamerica.org
http://www.opcofamerica.org

Visit this organization's Web site to access scholarship and internship information (for college students), high school journalism resources and programs (such as the High School Broadcast Journalism Project), useful publications, and salary and employment surveys. The association also offers membership to college students.

Radio Television Digital News Association
529 14th Street, NW, Suite 425
Washington, DC 20045-1406
Tel: 202-659-6510
http://www.rtdna.org

Visit the society's Web site for information on student chapters and scholarships for college students, job listings, training opportunities, educational resources, discussion boards and blogs, and much more.

Society of Professional Journalists
3909 North Meridian Street
Indianapolis, IN 46208-4011
Tel: 317-927-8000
http://www.spj.org

Visit the following Web site for comprehensive information on journalism careers, summer programs, and college journalism programs:

High School Journalism
http://www.highschooljournalism.org

INTERVIEW

Rick Pearson is a political reporter for the Chicago Tribune. *He discussed his career with the editors of* Careers in Focus: Politics.

Q. How long have you worked as a journalist? Why did you decide to become a political reporter?

A. I have been a journalist for more than three decades. I actually began my journalism career in high school when a friend, who worked for the school paper, noted that I attended all of the school's sports events and said the paper needed a sportswriter. I grew up with newspapers and actually learned to read at age three from the bold headlines the *Chicago Tribune* used on its front page. I studied how sportswriters at the *Tribune* and other papers wrote and the job at the school paper turned into a paid job writing sports for the regional twice-weekly newspaper. During college, I worked for a now-defunct paper in East St. Louis, covering all different kinds of stories. But after hearing sports clichés too many times, I enjoyed covering politicians who actually are involved in the policies and laws that govern us.

Q. What are the most important professional qualities for political reporters?

A. I believe there are several important professional qualities for political reporters. The first is honesty. That means reporting and writing a story without taking sides, without an agenda, without fear of stepping on the toes of the powerful. The story is the story. The second is to be fair. Politics is a business. Journalism is a business. Even if a politician doesn't like the story subject, they will grudgingly respect a reporter who offers to hear them out and present their side. Finally, political reporting should be accessible. I don't write for the insider. I write to inform the public of issues and personalities with which they should become familiar. I also write to try to explain the political motivations behind those pushing a policy agenda.

Q. What advice would you give to high school students who are interested in this career?

A. Since I grew up reading newspapers, writing was easy for me. But I would recommend anyone interested in writing for a career, even if it isn't journalism, to participate in their high school newspaper or yearbook classes and clubs. I would also suggest participating in the school's television or radio station if it has one. I spend almost as much of my time broadcasting as writing. One thing I didn't do in high school, but would recommend, in addition to a good foundation through writing classes, is possibly joining a debate team or club. Through a debate club, it's easy to see how politicians use the art of rhetoric to try to advance themselves and their positions, providing some strategic grounding for reporting on the subject.

Q. What has been one (or more) of your most rewarding experiences as a political reporter?

A. In working for more than three decades, I have had several rewarding experiences. As the lead political correspondent in Iowa in 1999, I chronicled the rise of George W. Bush to the presidency, covered his re-election, regularly rode aboard Air Force One, and was described by him as dressing "trendy" in a nationally broadcast news conference. At the same time, covering the Illinois legislature, I got to know a state senator in 1996 who went on to become a U.S. senator, and now president of the United States, named Barack Obama. I also was heavily involved in the coverage of the first Illinois governor to be impeached and removed from office, Rod Blagojevich, following federal charges of abuse of power and had written stories about the corruption investigations surrounding him after his first six months in office.

Political Scientists

OVERVIEW

Political scientists study the structure and theory of government, usually as part of an academic faculty. They are constantly seeking both theoretical and practical solutions to political problems. They divide their responsibilities between teaching and researching. After compiling facts, statistics, and other research, they present their analyses in reports, lectures, and journal articles. Approximately 4,100 political scientists are employed in the United States.

HISTORY

Political science is the oldest of the social sciences and is currently one of the most popular subjects of undergraduate study. The ideas of many early political scientists still influence current political theories: Machiavelli, the 16th-century Italian statesman and philosopher, believed that politics and morality are two entirely different spheres of human activity and that they should be governed by different standards and different laws; in the 17th century, Thomas Hobbes thought of government as a police force that prevented people from plundering their neighbors; John Locke was a 17th-century Englishman from whom we get the philosophy of "the greatest good for the greatest number." Some people call him the originator of "beneficent paternalism," which means that the state or ruler acts as a kindly leader to citizens, deciding what is best for them, then seeing that the "best" is put into effect, whether the citizens like it or not.

Common among theorists today is the assumption that politics is a process, the constant interaction of individuals and groups in

Notable Political Science Majors

Notable Figure	Position	Academic Institution
Earl Warren	United States Supreme Court justice	University of California, Berkeley
Jane Pauley	Television journalist	Indiana University
Mia Hamm	Professional soccer player (retired)	University of North Carolina
Steve Case	Founder of America Online	Williams College
Elizabeth Dole	Former U.S. Senator and former director of the American Red Cross	Duke University
Woodrow Wilson	28th president of the United States	Johns Hopkins University

activities that are directly or indirectly related to government. By 1945, political science in the United States was much more than the concern for institutions, law, formal structures of public government, procedures, and rules. It had expanded to include the dynamics of public governance. Instead of studying the rules of administrative procedure in a political group, for example, political scientists had begun to study the actual bureaucratic processes at work within the group. This signified the start of what would become systems theory in political science.

THE JOB

While many government careers involve taking action that directly affects political policy, political scientists study and discuss the results of these actions. "You can look into just about anything that interests you," says Chris Mooney, a professor in the political studies program at the University of Illinois at Springfield, "but you have to be able to argue that it's relevant to some basic theory in political science."

Political scientists may choose to research political lyrics in rock music, or study how teenagers form their political ideas. They may research the history of women in politics, the role of religion in politics, and the political histories of other countries. Many political scientists specialize in one area of study, such as public administration, history of political ideas, political parties, public law, American government, or international relations.

Some political scientists are employed as college and university professors. Depending on the institution for which they work, political scientists divide their time between teaching and researching.

In addition to teaching and researching, political scientists write books and articles based on their studies. A number of political science associations publish journals (such as *The American Political Science Review, Perspectives in Politics*, and *PS: Political Science and Politics)* and there are also small presses devoted to publishing works of political theory.

In researching policy issues, political scientists use a variety of different methods. They work with historians, economists, policy analysts, demographers, and statisticians. The Internet has become a very important resource tool for political scientists. The federal government has been dedicated to expanding the Internet, including making available full text of legislation, recent Supreme Court decisions, and access to the Library of Congress. Political scientists also use the data found in yearbooks and almanacs, material from encyclopedias, clippings from periodicals, or bound volumes of magazines or journals. They refer to law books, to statutes, to records of court cases, to the Congressional Record, and to other legislative records. They consult census records, historical documents, personal documents such as diaries and letters, and statistics from public opinion polls. They use libraries and archives to locate rare and old documents and records. For other information, political scientists use the "participant observer" method of research. In this method, they become part of a group and participate in its proceedings, while carefully observing interaction. They may also submit questionnaires. Questions will be carefully worded to elicit the facts needed, and the questionnaire will be administered to a selected sample of people.

When conducting research, political scientists must avoid letting their own biases distort the way in which they interpret the gathered facts. Then, they must compare their findings and analyses with those of others who have conducted similar investigations. Finally, they must present the data in an objective fashion, even though the findings may not reveal the kinds of facts they anticipated.

Those political scientists who are not employed as teachers work for labor unions, political organizations, or political interest groups.

Political scientists working for government may study organizations ranging in scope from the United Nations to local city councils. They may study the politics of a large city like New York or a small town in the Midwest. Their research findings may be used by a city's mayor and city council, to set public policy concerning waste management, or by an organization such as the National Organization for Women, to decide where to focus efforts on increasing the participation of women in local politics. Political scientists who work for the U.S. Department of State in either this country or in the Foreign Service use their analyses of political structures to make recommendations to the U.S. government concerning foreign policy.

Political scientists may also be employed by individual members of Congress. In this capacity, they might study government programs concerned with low-income housing and make recommendations to help the member of Congress write new legislation. Businesses and industries also hire political scientists to conduct polls on political issues that affect their operations. A tobacco company might want to know, for example, how the legislation restricting advertising by tobacco companies affects the buying habits of consumers of tobacco products.

REQUIREMENTS

High School
Take courses in government, American history, and civics to gain insight into politics. Math is also important because, as a political scientist, you will be evaluating statistics, demographics, and other numerical data. English and composition classes will help you develop the writing and communication skills you will need for teaching, publishing, and presenting papers. Take a journalism course and work for your high school newspaper to develop research, writing, and editing skills. Join a speech and debate team to gain experience researching current events, analyzing data, and presenting the information to others.

Postsecondary Training
Though you will be able to find some government jobs with a bachelor's degree in political science, you will not be able to pursue work in major academic institutions without a doctorate.

The American Political Science Association (APSA) publishes print and online directories of undergraduate and graduate political science programs and department chairpersons. An undergraduate program requires general courses in English, economics, statistics, and history, as well as courses in American politics, international politics, and political theory. Look for a school with a good internship program that can involve you with the U.S. Congress or a state legislature. *U.S. News and World Report* publishes rankings of graduate schools. In 2009 (the last year the magazine ranked schools in this discipline), Harvard (Cambridge, Massachusetts), Princeton (Princeton, New Jersey), and Stanford (Stanford, California) universities tied for first place.

Graduate study in political science includes courses in political parties, public opinion, comparative political behavior, and foreign policy design. You will also assist professors with research, attend conferences, write articles, and teach undergraduate courses.

Other Requirements
Because you will be compiling information from a number of different sources, you must be well organized. You should also enjoy reading and possess a curiosity about world politics. People skills are important, as you will be working closely with students and other political scientists. Other important traits include strong writing and research skills.

EXPLORING

Contact college political science departments for information about their programs. You can learn a lot about the work of a political scientist by looking at college course lists and faculty bios. Political science departments also have Web pages with information, and links to the curricula vitae of faculty. A curriculum vitae (C.V.) is an extensive resume, including lists of publications, conferences attended, and other professional experience. A C.V. can give you an idea of a political scientist's career and education path.

Contact the office of your state's senator or representative in the U.S. Congress about applying to work as a page. These highly competitive positions are available to students who are at least 16 years old. Pages serve members of Congress, running messages across Capitol Hill and handling many other support tasks. This experience is a valuable way to learn about the workings of government.

EMPLOYERS

Approximately 4,100 political scientists are employed in the United States. About 63 percent of political scientists work for the federal government. Political science is a popular major among undergraduates, so practically every college and university has a political science department. Political scientists find work at public and private universities, and at community colleges. They teach in undergraduate, master's, and doctoral programs. Teaching jobs at doctoral institutions are usually better paying and more prestigious. The most sought-after positions are those that offer tenure. Political scientists also work for companies that provide scientific research and development services and religious, civic, professional, grant making, and similar organizations.

STARTING OUT

Most graduate schools accept a very limited number of applicants every semester, so there's a lot of competition for admittance into some of the top programs. Applicants are admitted on the basis of grade point averages, test scores, internships performed, awards received, and other achievements.

Once you are in graduate school, you will begin to perform the work you will be doing in your career. You will teach undergraduate classes, attend conferences, present papers, and submit articles to political science journals. Your success as a graduate student will help you in your job search. After completing a graduate program, you will teach as an adjunct professor or visiting professor at various schools until you can find a permanent tenure-track position.

Membership in APSA and other political science associations entitles you to job placement assistance. APSA can also direct you to a number of fellowship and grant opportunities. Michigan State University posts humanities and social sciences job openings on its H-Net Job Guide Web page at http://www.h-net.org/jobs. Due to the heavy competition for these jobs, you will need an impressive C.V., including a list of publications in respected political science journals, a list of conferences attended, and good references attesting to your teaching skills.

ADVANCEMENT

In a tenure-track position, political scientists work their way up through the ranks from assistant professor to associate professor to full professor. They will probably have to work a few years in temporary, or visiting, faculty positions before they can join the permanent faculty of a political science department. They can then expect to spend approximately seven years working toward tenure. Tenure provides political scientists job security and prominence within their department and is awarded on the basis of publications, research performed, student evaluations, and teaching experience.

EARNINGS

The U.S. Department of Labor (DOL) reports that median annual earnings for political scientists were $104,090 in 2009. Salaries ranged from less than $46,520 to $151,360 or more. Starting federal government salaries for political scientists were $100,824 in March 2009.

Political science teachers employed at colleges and universities had mean annual earnings of $78,940 in 2009. Salaries ranged from less than $37,230 to $128,790 or more. Those employed at junior colleges earned mean annual salaries of $67,990.

Political scientists usually receive benefits such as vacation days, sick leave, health and life insurance, and a savings and pension program. Those who are self-employed must provide their own benefits.

WORK ENVIRONMENT

Political scientists who work as tenured faculty members enjoy pleasant surroundings. Depending on the size of the department, they will have their own office and be provided with a computer, Internet access, and research assistants. With good teaching skills, they will earn the respect of their students and colleagues.

Political science teachers work a fairly flexible schedule, teaching two or three courses a semester. The rest of their 40- to 50-hour workweek will be spent meeting individually with students, conducting research, writing, and serving on committees. Some travel may be required, as teachers attend a few conferences a year on behalf of their department, or as they take short-term assignments at other institutions. Teachers may teach some summer courses, or have the summer off. They will also have several days off between semesters.

OUTLOOK

Overall employment of social scientists is expected to grow faster than the average for all careers through 2018, according to the *Occupational Outlook Handbook*. The DOL predicts that demand for political scientists is growing because of "increasing interest in politics, foreign affairs, and public policy, including social and environmental policy issues, healthcare, and immigration."

The survival of political science departments depends on continued community and government support of education. The funding of humanities and social science programs is often threatened, resulting in budget cuts and hiring freezes. This makes for heavy competition for the few graduate assistantships and new faculty positions available. Also, there's not a great deal of mobility within the field; professors who achieve tenure generally stay in their positions until retirement.

More and more professors are using computers and the Internet, not just in research, but also in conducting their classes. According to an annual survey conducted by the Campus Computing Project, computers and CD-ROMs are used increasingly in the lecture hall, and many professors use the Internet to post class materials and other resources. Some classes are held entirely online.

FOR MORE INFORMATION

To read about the issues affecting college professors, contact
American Association of University Professors
1133 19th Street, NW, Suite 200
Washington, DC 20036-3655
Tel: 202-737-5900
E-mail: aaup@aaup.org
http://www.aaup.org

For more information on careers, useful publications, educational programs, and graduate school, contact
American Political Science Association
1527 New Hampshire Avenue, NW
Washington, DC 20036-1206
Tel: 202-483-2512
E-mail: apsa@apsanet.org
http://www.apsanet.org

For career information, contact
National Conference of Black Political Scientists
http://www.ncobps.org

For employment opportunities, mail your resume and a cover letter to
Senate Placement Office
SH-116, Hart Senate Office Building
Washington DC 20510-0001

Tel: 202-224-9167
E-mail: placementofficeinfo@saa.senate.gov
http://www.senate.gov/employment

U.S. House of Representatives
Office of Human Resources
102 Ford House Office Building
Washington, DC 20515-0001
Tel: 202-226-4504
http://www.house.gov/cao-hr

Political Speechwriters

OVERVIEW

Political speechwriters prepare speeches for individuals in the political arena. They write for politicians in all branches of government, from the local and state level to the national level, including the president of the United States.

HISTORY

History is filled with politicians who were renowned as great orators. But what about those who helped them write their compelling and memorable speeches? Undoubtedly, all politicians have had some help with writing their speeches through history. The first president of the United States, George Washington, is said to have received help with his speeches from Alexander Hamilton, the first secretary of the U.S. Department of the Treasury. A gentleman by the name of Judson Welliver is generally considered to be the first person employed as a speechwriter for a U.S. president, serving Calvin Coolidge in the 1920s. Nowadays, full-time speechwriters employed in the official White House Office of Speechwriting help the president craft memorable speeches. Presidents are not the only ones who sometimes need help creating a captivating and inspiring speech—politicians at every level and branch of government utilize speechwriters to communicate their ideas to a variety of audiences.

THE JOB

Political speechwriters write speeches for politicians, or they may assist the politician in composing a speech. A politician may need speechwriters for several reasons. Many politicians are extremely busy and simply do not have the time to write the many speeches they need to give. Others may not feel comfortable writing their own speeches and require the presence of a speechwriter to help them make sense of what they want to say, and how they want to convey that message in a speech. Still other politicians may have excellent ideas for their speeches but need help communicating their vision to others.

A political speechwriter usually begins writing a speech once a topic is selected. They may have a topic assigned to them, or they may have to determine the topic of the speech themselves. To do this, a speechwriter may meet with the politician who they are writing for to receive his or her input. A speechwriter might also meet with representatives of the group the politician will be speaking to, in order to discover their concerns and ensure that they are addressed in the speech. Next, the speechwriter will typically research the topic to be mentioned in the speech. To do this, they may utilize the resources of libraries, the Internet, or interview knowledgeable authorities in the field.

Once a speechwriter has gathered enough initial information, they begin to write the speech. Speechwriters must keep several things in mind while writing the speech. They need to make sure the speech sounds like it was written by the politician who will ultimately be delivering it. They also need to keep in mind who will be hearing the speech, making sure that the speech is written in a way that it will be not only understood by the intended audience, but that it will also prove to be persuasive and effective in delivering the politician's message. The speechwriter is also concerned with the mechanics of good speechwriting: allowing the speaker to engage the audience; providing clear, key points of the speech that can be easily recognized and digested by the audience; and making sure the audience identifies positively with the speaker by the end of the speech. They also have to be concerned with more mundane issues, such as making sure the speech does not exceed any time limits that have been set.

After the speechwriter finishes a rough draft of a speech, it will need to be approved by the politician delivering it. Depending on the individual, he or she may or may not have had any interaction with the speechwriter until this stage. The politician, as well as their advisers, may revise the speech and send it back to the speechwriter for additional work, changing anything the politician or advisers are not satisfied or comfortable with. At this point, the speech may be shuffled back and forth several more times before it is finally approved.

Political Speeches on the Web

Visit the following Web sites to read and listen to famous political speeches:

American Rhetoric: Online Speech Bank
http://www.americanrhetoric.com/speechbank.htm

Gifts of Speech: Women's Speeches From Around the World
http://gos.sbc.edu

Speech Wall
http://www.speechwall.com

After the speech is approved, the speechwriter may be responsible for producing the speech in its final form, which varies across different situations. The speech may need to be typed on easily readable note cards for a politician speaking in a small auditorium, or the speech might need to be on a computer disk that can be input into a TelePrompTer and displayed on a monitor for the politician to read at a large rally or televised event.

REQUIREMENTS

High School

Since speechwriters need to be strong communicators, you should take as many English, speech, and communications courses as you can. Take courses in civics, history, and government as well. If possible, join a speech or debate team to gain experience researching current events, analyzing data, and presenting information to others.

Postsecondary Training

You will need a bachelor's degree, preferably in a field related to communications or political science, to become a political speechwriter. In addition to taking as many writing, speech, and communications classes as you can, you should pursue a well-rounded education, taking courses in history and politics.

Other Requirements

To be a successful speechwriter, you must stay up-to-date with current events and daily news. You must be flexible and able to integrate late-breaking news items into speeches you have written. You must also be able to work under pressure and meet deadlines. Because speechwriters need to interact with others, you should have good people skills.

EXPLORING

The best way to find out if speechwriting is something you wish to pursue is to write—anything—as often as possible. The more you write, the more you will improve your skills. You can practice writing speeches on your own, or you can participate with your school's speech or debate teams. Join local groups to learn the basics of effective public speaking so you can write more successful speeches. Reading famous speeches will also help you to understand the components of a successful speech. You can also join nonprofit or political organizations and offer to assist with public speaking events. This will give you the opportunity to make contacts, observe their operations, and you might even get an opportunity to assist a speechwriter with research. You might also consider starting your own online blog. In this setting, you can write about anything that comes to your mind, and receive feedback from readers.

EMPLOYERS

Most political speechwriters work for politicians or political consulting groups. Many jobs are in Washington, D.C., but there are opportunities available across the nation at the state and local government levels. One thing to keep in mind: It can be very difficult to write speeches supporting issues that go against your own views or morals. If you find employment with a politician who is closely aligned with your own opinions on issues that are important to you, your job will be easier and have the potential to be very rewarding.

STARTING OUT

One of the most important and effective ways of getting started as a political speechwriter is to make connections with people involved in politics. Volunteer for political campaigns and be an advocate of public policy issues that interest you. You can make good connections, and gain valuable experience, working or interning in the offices of your state capital. You might also try for an internship with one of your state's members of Congress; contact their offices in Washington, D.C., for internship applications.

Some people pursue a career as a political speechwriter directly by working in the press offices of political candidates, starting out as assistants to speechwriters or press secretaries, advancing as they are able to demonstrate their ability and as opportunities arise. Others make the jump to speechwriting after having worked in the political arena as lawyers, lobbyists, or journalists.

ADVANCEMENT

Political speechwriters have many advancement options. Entry-level speechwriters may progress from doing mostly research, to writing some low-profile speeches, to writing more important speeches. They may also start by working with politicians at the local level and move on to work with higher-level politicians at the state or national levels. Or they may find themselves promoted to speechwriting positions that have more supervisory and organizational responsibilities, such as managing a team of speechwriters.

Some political speechwriters advance to non-speechwriting positions within public administration; for example, they may become politicians or political consultants. They may also make the transition to a career in media, finding employment as a writer, journalist, or a career in public relations.

EARNINGS

Median annual salaries for all writers were $53,900 in 2009, according to the U.S. Department of Labor (DOL). Salaries ranged from less than $28,070 to $105,710 or more. Mean annual salaries for writers employed by the federal government were $81,120. Entry-level speechwriters typically earn around $20,000, and experienced speechwriters who work with high-profile politicians may make considerably more, earning salaries of $125,000 or more. Salaries also depend on geographical location and the level of government or politician for which the speechwriter writes.

Benefits for salaried speechwriters depend on the employer; however, they usually include such items as health insurance, retirement or 401(k) plans, and paid vacation days. Self-employed speechwriters must provide their own benefits.

WORK ENVIRONMENT

The work environment of political speechwriters can vary. At times, they may find themselves working in a relatively quiet office. They may also find themselves traveling on a crowded bus, train, or plane with the politician for whom they are writing, trying to craft a speech that needs to be finished by the time they arrive at their next destination. Work hours in this profession can be long and very irregular. This is especially the case when a speechwriter is working for a major political candidate on the campaign trail.

The work environment, whether it is on the road or in the office, has the potential to be frantic, noisy, and stressful. Politicians, political advisers, and speechwriters may have opposing views of what needs to be included in a speech, leading to heated exchanges. Speechwriters may have to make last-minute changes to a speech based on the day's news events, all with the stress of deadlines looming. That said, not all speechwriters are employed in these high-pressured settings. Depending on their employer, a speechwriter may also work in a typical office environment, with fairly regular work hours.

OUTLOOK

The DOL does not provide employment outlook information for the career of political speechwriter. It is safe to say, though, given the prevalence of politics and the importance of effective communication in the world today, that political speechwriters will have steady employment opportunities for the next decade.

FOR MORE INFORMATION

This organization provides professional guidance, assistance, and education to members and maintains a code of ethics.
American Association of Political Consultants
8400 Westpark Drive, 2nd Floor
McLean, VA 22102-5116
Tel: 703-245-8020
http://www.theaapc.org

Visit the Web sites of the House and the Senate for press releases and links to sites for individual members of Congress to inquire about internship opportunities. To write to your state's representatives, contact
U.S. House of Representatives
Office of the Honorable (Name)
Washington, DC 20510-0001
Tel: 202-224-3121
http://www.house.gov

U.S. Senate
Office of Senator (Name)
Washington, DC 20510-0001
Tel: 202-224-3121
http://www.senate.gov

To gain insight into effective public speaking, contact
Toastmasters International
PO Box 9052
Mission Viejo, CA 92690-9052
Tel: 949-858-8255
http://www.toastmasters.org

Press Secretaries and Political Consultants

OVERVIEW

Press secretaries, political consultants, and other media relations professionals help politicians promote themselves and their issues among voters. They advise politicians on how to address the media. Sometimes called *spin doctors*, these professionals use the media to either change or strengthen public opinion. Press secretaries work for candidates and elected officials, while political consultants work with firms, contracting their services to politicians. The majority of press secretaries and political consultants work in Washington, D.C.; others work all across the country, involved with local and state government officials and candidates.

HISTORY

The practice of using the media for political purposes is nearly as old as the U.S. government itself. The news media developed right alongside the political parties, and early newspapers served as a battleground for the Federalists and the Republicans. The first media moguls of the late 1800s often saw their newspapers as podiums from which to promote themselves. George Hearst bought the *San Francisco Examiner* in 1885 for the sole purpose of helping him campaign for Congress.

The latter half of the 20th century introduced whole other forms of media, which were quickly exploited by politicians seeking offices. Many historians mark the Kennedy-Nixon debate of 1960 as the moment when television coverage first became a key factor in the

Women in Politics

Although women make up more than 50 percent of the U.S. population, they are vastly underrepresented in the halls of Congress and at other levels of government. In 2010, according to the Center for American Women and Politics, women made up:

- 16.8 percent of the House of Representatives
- 17 percent of the Senate
- 12 percent of U.S. governors
- 24.4 percent of state legislatures

Despite these statistics, women today are actually enjoying their largest representation ever in the political arena. Elected and appointed leaders such as Olympia Snowe (U.S. senator), Jennifer Granholm (governor of Michigan), Lisa Madigan (attorney general of Illinois), Christine Gregoire (governor of Washington), Nancy Pelosi (speaker of the House of Representatives), and Hillary Clinton (U.S. Secretary of State) are proving that women can handle the stress and demands of government service.

What is the next step for women in elected office? Increased representation at all levels of government, and more importantly, the election of the first female president of the United States. Is this dream out of the question? No, if you believe a recent poll of American voters. According to a February 2007 survey by Roper Public Affairs, 74 percent of Americans say they would feel comfortable with a female president.

The White House Project, a national, nonpartisan organization that is dedicated to advancing the role of women in all positions of leadership, offers a variety of useful resources to encourage women to enter politics and attain other positions of leadership. For more information, visit http://www.thewhitehouseproject.org.

election process. Those who read of the debate in the next day's newspapers were under the impression that Nixon had easily won, but it was Kennedy's composure and appeal on camera that made the most powerful impression. Negative campaigning first showed its powerful influence in 1964, when Democratic presidential candidate Lyndon Johnson ran ads featuring a girl picking a flower while a nuclear bomb exploded in the background, which commented on Republican candidate Barry Goldwater's advocacy of strong military action in Vietnam.

Bill Clinton is an example of a politician who benefited from the art of "spin," as his press secretaries and political managers were actively involved in dealing with his scandals and keeping his approval ratings high among the public. James Carville and George Stephanopoulos, working for Clinton's 1992 campaign, had the task of playing up Clinton's strengths as an intelligent, gifted politician, while downplaying questionable events in his personal life. Their efforts were portrayed in the documentary *The War Room*, and their success earned them national renown as "spin doctors."

THE JOB

If you were to manage a political campaign, how would you go about publicizing the candidate to the largest number of voters? You would use television, of course. The need for TV and radio spots during a campaign is the reason it costs so much today to run for office. And it's also the reason many politicians hire professionals with an understanding of media relations to help them get elected. Once elected, a politician continues to rely on media relations experts, such as press secretaries, political consultants, and political managers, to use the media to portray the politician in the best light. In recent years, such words as *spin*, *leak*, and *sound bite* have entered the daily vocabulary of news and politics to describe elements of political coverage in the media.

Political consultants usually work independently, or as members of consulting firms, and contract with individuals. Political consultants are involved in producing radio and TV ads, writing campaign plans, and developing themes for these campaigns. A theme may focus on a specific issue or on the differences between the client and the opponent. Their client may be new to the political arena or someone established looking to maintain an office. They conduct polls and surveys to gauge public opinion and to identify their client's biggest competition. Political consultants advise their clients in the best ways to use the media. In addition to TV and radio, the Internet has proven important to politicians. Consultants launch campaign Web sites, manage a politician's postings on microblogging sites such as Twitter, and also chase down rumors that spread across the Internet. A consultant may be hired for an entire campaign, or may be hired only to produce an ad, or to come up with a sound bite (or catchy quote) for the media.

Though voters across the country complain about negative campaigning, or "mudslinging," such campaigns have proven effective. In his 1988 presidential campaign, George H. W. Bush ran TV ads featuring the now notorious Willie Horton, a convict who was released from prison only to commit another crime. The ad was intended to draw attention to what Bush considered his opponent's soft approach to crime. It proved very effective in undermining the campaign of Michael Dukakis and putting him on the defensive. Many consultants believe they must focus on a few specific issues in a campaign, emphasizing their client's strengths as well as the opponent's weaknesses.

Press secretaries serve on the congressional staffs of senators and representatives and on the staffs of governors and mayors. The president also has a press secretary. Press secretaries and their assistants write press releases and opinion pieces to publicize the efforts of the government officials for whom they work. They also help prepare speeches and prepare their employers for press conferences and interviews. They maintain Web sites, posting press releases and the results of press conferences.

Media relations experts are often called spin doctors because of their ability to manipulate the media, or put a good spin on a news story to best suit the purposes of their clients. Corporations also rely on spin for positive media coverage. Media relations experts are often called upon during a political scandal, or after corporate blunders, for damage control. Using the newspapers, the Internet, and

Former White House Press Secretary Robert Gibbs speaks during a daily briefing at the White House. *(Susan Walsh, AP Photo)*

radio and TV broadcasts, spin doctors attempt to downplay public relations disasters, helping politicians and corporations save face. In highly sensitive situations, they must answer questions selectively and carefully, and they may even be involved in secretly releasing, or leaking, information to the press. Because of these manipulations, media relations professionals are often disrespected. They are sometimes viewed as people who conceal facts and present lies, prey on the emotions of voters, or even represent companies responsible for illegal practices. However, many political consultants and media representatives are responsible for bringing public attention to important issues and good political candidates. They also help organizations and nonprofit groups advocate for legislative issues and help develop support for school funding, environmental concerns, and other community needs.

REQUIREMENTS

High School
English composition, drama, and speech classes will help you develop good communication skills, while government, history, and civics classes will teach you about the structure of local, state, and federal government. Take math, economics, and accounting courses to prepare for poll-taking and for analyzing statistics and demographics.

While in high school, work with your school newspaper, radio station, TV station, or journalism Web site. This will help you recognize how important reporters, editors, and producers are in putting together newspapers and shaping news segments. You should also consider joining your school's speech and debate team to gain experience in research and in persuasive argument.

Postsecondary Training
Most people in media relations have bachelor's degrees, and some also hold master's degrees, doctorates, and law degrees. As an undergraduate, you should enroll in a four-year college and pursue a well-rounded education. Press secretaries and political consultants need a good understanding of the history and culture of the United States and foreign countries. Some of the majors you should consider as an undergraduate are journalism, political science, English, marketing, and economics. You should take courses in government, psychology, statistics, history of western civilization, and a foreign language. You might then choose to pursue a graduate degree in journalism, political science, public administration, or international relations.

Seek a college with a good internship program. You might also pursue internships with local and state officials and your congressional members in the Senate and House of Representatives. Journalism internships will involve you with local and national publications, or the news departments of radio and TV stations.

Certification or Licensing
There is no certification or licensing available for press secretaries and political consultants. The Public Relations Society of America and the International Association of Business Communicators accredit public relations workers in the private sector who have at least five years of experience in the field and pass a comprehensive examination. Such accreditation is a sign of competence in this field, although it is not a requirement for employment.

Other Requirements
In this career, you need to be very organized and capable of juggling many different tasks, from quickly writing ads and press releases to developing budgets and expense accounts. You need good problem-solving skills and some imagination when putting a positive spin on negative issues. Good people skills are important so that you can develop contacts within government and the media. You should feel comfortable with public speaking, leading press conferences, and speaking on behalf of your employers and clients. You should also enjoy competition. You can't be intimidated by people in power or by journalists questioning the issues addressed in your campaigns.

EXPLORING

Get involved with your school government as well as with committees and clubs that have officers and elections. You can also become involved in local, state, and federal elections by volunteering for campaigns; though you may just be making phone calls and putting up signs, you may also have the opportunity to write press releases and schedule press conferences and interviews, and you will see firsthand how a campaign operates.

Working for your school newspaper will help you learn about conducting research, interviews, and opinion polls, which all play a part in managing media relations. You may be able to get a part-time job or an internship with your city's newspaper or broadcast news station, where you will gain experience with election coverage and political advertising. Visit the Web sites of U.S. Congress members. Many sites feature lists of recent press releases, which will give you a sense of how a press office publicizes the efforts and actions of Congress members. Read some of the many books examining recent political campaigns and scandals, and read magazines like *Harper's* (http://www.harpers.org), *The Economist* (http://www .economist.com), *The Atlantic* (http://www.theatlantic.com), and the online magazine Salon.com (http://www.salon.com) for political commentary.

EMPLOYERS

Though a majority of press secretaries and political consultants work in Washington, D.C., others work in state capitals and major cities all across the country. Press secretaries work for local, state, and federal government officials. They also find work with public relations agencies, and the press offices of large corporations. Celebrities, and others in the public eye also hire press agents to help them control rumors and publicity.

Political consultants are generally self-employed, or work for consulting firms that specialize in media relations. They contract with politicians, corporations, nonprofit groups, and trade and professional associations. They participate in the campaigns of mayors, governors, and Congress members as well as in the political campaigns of other countries.

STARTING OUT

Media relations jobs aren't advertised, and there is no predetermined path to success. It is recommended that you make connections with people in both politics and the media. Volunteer for political campaigns, and also advocate for public policy issues of interest to you. You can make good connections, and gain valuable experience, working or interning in the offices of your state capital. You might also try for an internship with one of your state's members of Congress; contact their offices in Washington, D.C., for internship applications. If you're more interested in the writing and producing aspects of the career, work for local newspapers or the broadcast news media; or work as a producer for a television production crew or for an ad agency that specializes in political campaigns. A political consulting firm may hire assistants for writing and for commercial production. Whereas some people pursue the career directly by working in the press offices of political candidates, others find their way into political consulting after having worked as lawyers, lobbyists, or journalists.

ADVANCEMENT

A press secretary who has worked closely with a successful government official may advance into a higher staff position, like chief of staff or legislative director. Political consultants, after winning many elections and establishing credentials, will begin to take on more prominent clients and major campaigns. Network TV, cable, and radio news departments also hire successful media relations experts to serve as political analysts on the air. Some consultants also write columns for newspapers and syndicates and publish books about their insights into politics.

EARNINGS

According to the U.S. Department of Labor (DOL), public relations specialists (a career category that includes press secretaries) had median annual earnings of $51,960 in 2009, with salaries ranging from less than $30,520 to more than $96,630. In 2009, mean earnings for those who worked in local government were $54,720.

Public relations managers had annual earnings of $47,800 to $166,400 or more in 2009, with median annual earnings of $89,690. Those who work for local government had mean annual earnings of $79,130 in 2009, according to the DOL.

According to the Congressional Management Foundation (CMF), a nonprofit organization in Washington, D.C., press secretaries working in the U.S. House of Representatives earned less than their counterparts in the Senate. The CMF found that the average pay of a House press secretary was $45,301, while those employed by the Senate earned an average of $116,573. This pay differential is probably even greater, because the CMF info for the Senate is from 1999, while the House data is from 2000, which is the most recent information available.

The incomes of political consultants vary greatly. Someone contracting with local candidates, or with state organizations and associations, may make around $40,000 a year; someone consulting with high-profile candidates may earn hundreds of thousands of dollars a year.

Benefits for press secretaries and political consultants depend on the employer; however, they usually include such items as health insurance, retirement or 401(k) plans, and paid vacation days. Self-employed workers must provide their own benefits.

WORK ENVIRONMENT

Representing politicians can be thankless work. Press secretaries may have to speak to the press about sensitive, volatile issues and deal directly with the frustrations of journalists unable to get the answers they want. When working for prominent politicians, they may become the subject of personal attacks.

Despite these potential conflicts, the work can be exciting and fast-paced. Press secretaries and political consultants see the results of their efforts in the newspapers and on television, and they have the satisfaction of influencing voters and public opinion. If working on a campaign as a consultant, their hours will be long and stressful. In some cases, they'll have to scrap unproductive media ads and start from scratch with only hours to write, produce, and place new commercials. They will also have to be available to their clients around the clock.

OUTLOOK

Employment for press secretaries and political consultants is expected to be good during the next decade. Consultants and media representatives will become increasingly important to candidates and elected officials. Television ads and Internet campaigns have become almost necessary to reach the public. The work of press secretaries will expand as more news networks, news magazines, and political Web sites closely follow the decisions and actions of government officials.

The Pew Research Center for the People and the Press, which surveys public opinion on political issues, has found that most Americans are concerned about negative campaigning, while most political consultants see nothing wrong with using negative tactics in advertising. Despite how the general public may feel about negative campaigning, it remains a very effective tool for consultants. In some local elections, candidates may mutually agree to avoid the mudslinging, but the use of negative ads in general is likely to increase.

This negative campaigning may be affected somewhat by developing technology. Voters are now able to access more information about candidates and issues via the Internet. Also, the increase in the number of channels available to cable TV viewers makes it more difficult for candidates to advertise to a general audience. However, the greater number of outlets for media products will create an increased demand for writers, TV producers, and Web designers to help candidates reach potential voters.

FOR MORE INFORMATION

This organization provides professional guidance, assistance, and education to members and maintains a code of ethics.

American Association of Political Consultants
8400 Westpark Drive, 2nd Floor
McLean, VA 22102-5116
Tel: 703-245-8020
http://www.theaapc.org

The association provides information on broadcast education, scholarships for college students, jobs, and useful publications at its Web site.

National Association of Broadcasters
1771 N Street, NW
Washington, DC 20036-2800
Tel: 202-429-5300
E-mail: nab@nab.org
http://www.nab.org

The Pew Research Center is an opinion research group that studies attitudes toward press, politics, and public policy issues. To read some of its survey results, visit its Web site or contact

The Pew Research Center for the People and the Press
1615 L Street, NW, Suite 700
Washington, DC 20036-5621
Tel: 202-419-4350
http://www.people-press.org

Visit the Web sites of the House and the Senate for press releases and links to sites for individual members of Congress. To write to your state representatives, contact

U.S. House of Representatives
Office of the Honorable (Name)
Washington, DC 20510-0001
Tel: 202-224-3121
http://www.house.gov

U.S. Senate
Office of Senator (Name)
Washington, DC 20510-0001
Tel: 202-224-3121
http://www.senate.gov

Public Opinion Researchers

OVERVIEW

Public opinion researchers employed in politics help measure public sentiment about a particular politician or social issues (such as affirmative action, health care reform, or immigration) by gathering information from a sample of the population through questionnaires and interviews. They are also called *pollsters* and *polling analysts*. They collect, analyze, and interpret data and opinions to explore issues and forecast trends. Their poll results help politicians determine what's on the public's mind.

HISTORY

Public opinion research began in a rudimentary way in the 1830s and 1840s when local newspapers asked their readers to fill out unofficial ballots indicating for whom they had voted in a particular election. Since that time, research on political issues has been conducted with increasing frequency—especially during presidential election years. A large amount of money is spent to gather information. In fact, the Council of American Survey Research Organizations reports that "the U.S. federal system, including such agencies as the Bureau of the Census, spends approximately $4 billion annually on economic and social information collected through surveys and employs over 12,000 staff."

As questionnaires and interviewing techniques have become more refined, the field of public opinion research has become more accurate at reflecting the individual attitudes and opinions of the

QUICK FACTS

School Subjects
Mathematics
Psychology

Personal Skills
Communication/ideas
Technical/scientific

Work Environment
Indoors and outdoors
Primarily multiple locations

Minimum Education Level
Bachelor's degree

Salary Range
$17,860 to $61,580 to
$111,900+

Certification or Licensing
Voluntary

Outlook
Much faster than the average

DOT
205

GOE
02.04.02

NOC
1454

O*NET-SOC
19-3021.00, 19-3022.00

sample groups. Companies like Gallup Inc. and Harris Interactive conduct surveys for a wide range of political and economic purposes. Although some people continue to question the accuracy and importance of polls, they have become an integral part of our social fabric and a key tool for politicians and government agencies.

THE JOB

Public opinion researchers conduct interviews and gather data that accurately reflect public opinions. They do this so politicians and government agencies have a better idea of what people want on a wide range of issues. Public opinion is sometimes gauged by interviewing a small percentage of the population containing a variety of people who closely parallel the larger population in terms of age, race, income, and other factors. At other times, researchers interview people who represent a certain demographic group or political party. Public opinion researchers, for example, may help a political candidate decide which campaign issues the public considers important.

Researchers use a variety of methods to collect and analyze public opinion. The particular method depends on the target audience and the type of information desired. For example, if a political organization is interested in gauging the opinions of a cross-section of American voters, the research company will most likely station interviewers in selected areas around a mall or outside a grocery store so they can question people. On the other hand, an elected official may be interested in the opinions of a particular demographic group, such as working mothers or independent voters. In this case, the research firm would plan a procedure (such as a telephone survey) providing access to that group. Other field collection methods include interviews in the home and at work as well as questionnaires that are filled out by respondents and then returned through the mail.

Planning is an important ingredient in developing an effective survey method. After they receive an assignment, researchers decide what portion of the population they will survey and develop questions that will result in an accurate gauging of opinion. Researchers investigate whether previous surveys have been done on a particular topic, and if so, what the results were.

It is important that exactly the same procedures be used throughout the entire data collection process so that the survey is not influenced by the individual styles of the interviewers. For this reason, the process is closely monitored by supervisory personnel. *Research assistants* help train survey interviewers, prepare survey questionnaires and related materials, and tabulate and code survey results.

Survey workers conduct public opinion interviews to determine people's opinions on public issues. Survey workers contact people in their homes, at work, at random in public places, or via the telephone, questioning the person in a specified manner, usually following a questionnaire format.

REQUIREMENTS

High School
Because the ability to communicate in both spoken and written form is crucial for this job, you should take courses in English, speech arts, and social studies while in high school. In addition, take mathematics (especially statistics), political science, and any courses in journalism or psychology that are available. Knowledge of a foreign language is also helpful.

Postsecondary Training
A college degree in economics or business administration provides a good background for public opinion researchers. A degree in political science or government will be helpful for those interested in working in the field of politics.

Because of the increasingly sophisticated techniques used in public opinion research, most employers expect researchers to be familiar with computer applications, and many require a master's degree in business administration, sociology, educational psychology, or political science. While a doctorate is not necessary for most researchers, it is highly desirable for those who plan to become involved with complex research studies or work in an academic environment.

Certification or Licensing
The Marketing Research Association and the American Marketing Association offer certification for marketing research analysts (a type of public opinion researcher). Contact these organizations for more information.

Other Requirements
Public opinion researchers who conduct interviews must be outgoing and enjoy interacting with a wide variety of people. Because much of the work involves getting people to reveal their personal opinions and beliefs, you must be a good listener and as nonjudgmental as possible. You must be patient and be able to handle rejection because some people may be uncooperative during the interviewing process.

If you choose to work in data analysis, you should be able to pay close attention to detail and spend long hours analyzing complex data. You may experience some pressure when forced to collect data or solve a problem within a specified period of time. If you intend to plan questionnaires, you will need good analytical skills and a strong command of the English language.

EXPLORING

High school students can often work as survey workers for a tele-marketing firm or other consumer research company. Work opportunities may also be available where you can learn about the coding and tabulation of survey data. Actual participation in a consumer survey may also offer insight into the type of work involved in the field. You should also try to talk with professionals already working in the field to learn more about the profession.

EMPLOYERS

Public opinion workers who work in politics are employed by individual candidates, political parties, or by government agencies. Others work for international organizations such as the United Nations and the World Health Organization. Many public opinion researchers are employed by private companies, such as public and private research firms and advertising agencies. They also work for colleges and universities, often in research and teaching capacities.

STARTING OUT

Many people enter the field in a support position such as a survey worker, and with experience become interviewers or work as data analysts. Those with applicable education, training, and experience may begin as interviewers or data analysts. College career services counselors can often help qualified students find an appropriate position in public opinion research. Contacts can also be made through summer employment or by locating public and private research companies in the phone book or on the Internet. Those who are interested in working in politics should contact political candidates, political parties, or government agencies directly for information on employment opportunities.

ADVANCEMENT

Advancement opportunities are numerous in the public opinion research field. Often a research assistant will be promoted to a position as an interviewer or data analyst and, after sufficient experience in these or other aspects of research project development, become involved in a supervisory or planning capacity.

With a master's degree or doctorate, a person can become a manager of a large private research organization. Those with extended work experience in public opinion research and with sufficient credentials may choose to start their own companies. Opportunities also exist in university teaching or research and development.

EARNINGS

Starting salaries vary according to the skill and experience of the applicant, the nature of the position, the size of the organization, and other factors. The U.S. Department of Labor (DOL) does not offer salary information for public opinion researchers. It does report that market research analysts (a type of public opinion researcher) earned median annual salaries of $61,580 in 2009. Earnings ranged from less than $34,260 to $111,900 or more. Market research analysts who worked for the federal government earned mean annual salaries of $90,010. The department also reports that survey workers earned salaries that ranged from less than $17,860 to more than $76,710 in 2009. The median annual salary for survey workers was $35,380 in 2009. Those in academic positions may earn somewhat less than their counterparts in the business community, but federal government salaries are competitive with those in the private sector.

Most full-time public opinion researchers receive the usual medical, pension, vacation, and other benefits that other professional workers do. Managers may also receive bonuses based on their company's performance.

WORK ENVIRONMENT

Public opinion researchers usually work a standard 40-hour week, although they may have to work overtime occasionally if a project has a tight deadline. Those in supervisory positions may work especially long hours overseeing the collection and interpretation of information.

When conducting telephone interviews or organizing or analyzing data, researchers work in comfortable offices, with calculators, computers, and data processing equipment close at hand. When collecting information via personal interviews or questionnaires, it is not unusual to spend time outside in shopping malls, on the street, or in private homes. Some evening and weekend work may be involved because people are most readily available to be interviewed at those times. Some research positions may include assignments that involve travel, but these are generally short assignments.

OUTLOOK

According to the DOL, employment of market and survey research workers is expected to grow much faster than the average for all occupations through 2018. As is usually the case, those with the most experience and education (particularly those with graduate degrees) should find the greatest number of job opportunities.

FOR MORE INFORMATION

For information on graduate programs, contact
American Association for Public Opinion Research
111 Deer Lake Road, Suite 100
Deerfield, IL 60015-4943
Tel: 847-205-2651
E-mail: info@aapor.org
http://www.aapor.org

For information on political consulting, contact
American Association of Political Consultants
8400 Westpark Drive, 2nd Floor
McLean, VA 22102-5116
Tel: 703-245-8020
http://www.theaapc.org

For information on survey research and graduate programs, contact
Council of American Survey Research Organizations
170 North Country Road, Suite 4
Port Jefferson, NY 11777-2606
Tel: 631-928-6954
E-mail: casro@casro.org
http://www.casro.org

For information on the collection of statistics for federal government agencies, contact
Council of Professional Associations on Federal Statistics
2121 Eisenhower Avenue, Suite 200
Alexandria, VA 22314-4688
Tel: 703-836-0404
http://www.copafs.org

For information on public polls, contact
The National Council on Public Polls
Tel: 202-293-4710
E-mail: info@ncpp.org
http://www.ncpp.org

The Pew Research Center is an opinion research group that studies attitudes toward press, politics, and public policy issues. To read some of its survey results, visit its Web site or contact
The Pew Research Center for the People and the Press
1615 L Street, NW, Suite 700
Washington, DC 20036-5621
Tel: 202-419-4350
http://www.people-press.org

For information on careers in survey research, visit
Careers Outside the Box
http://www.casro.org/careers

The following companies are leaders in survey and marketing research:
Gallup Inc.
http://www.gallup.com

Harris Interactive
http://www.harrisinteractive.com

Regional and Local Officials

OVERVIEW

Regional and local officials hold positions in the legislative, executive, and judicial branches of government at the local level. They include mayors, commissioners, and city and county council members. These officials direct regional legal services, public health departments, and police protection. They serve on housing, budget, and employment committees and develop special programs to improve communities.

HISTORY

The first U.S. colonies adopted the English shire form of government. This form was 1,000 years old and served as the administrative arm of both the national and local governments; a county in medieval England was overseen by a sheriff (originally a shire reeve) appointed by the crown and was represented by two members in Parliament.

When America's founding fathers composed the Constitution, they didn't make any specific provisions for the governing of cities and counties. This allowed state governments to compose their own definitions; when drawing up their own constitutions, the states essentially considered county governments to be extensions of the state government. City governments, necessary for dealing with increased industry and trade, evolved during the 19th century. Population growth and suburban development helped to strengthen local governments after World War I. The county governments grew even stronger after World War II, due to rising revenues and increased independence from the states.

Most Populous Cities

1. New York City, N.Y. (8,391,881 people)
2. Los Angeles, Calif. (3,831,868)
3. Chicago, Ill. (2,851,268)
4. Houston, Tex. (2,257,926)
5. Phoenix, Ariz. (1,601,587)
6. Philadelphia, Pa. (1,547,297)
7. San Antonio, Tex. (1,373,668)
8. San Diego, Calif. (1,306,301)
9. Dallas, Tex. (1,299,543)
10. San Jose, Calif. (964,695)

Source: U.S. Census Bureau (rankings as of 7/1/09)

THE JOB

There are a variety of different forms of local government across the country, but they all share similar concerns. County and city governments make sure that the local streets are free of crime as well as free of potholes. They create and improve regional parks and organize music festivals and outdoor theater events to be staged in these parks. They identify community problems and help to solve them in original ways. For example, in an effort to solve the problem of unemployment among those recently released from jail, King County in Washington State developed a baking training program for county inmates. The inmates' new talents with danishes and bread loaves opened up good-paying job opportunities in grocery store bakeries all across the county. King County also has many youth programs, including the Paul Robeson Scholar-Athlete Award to recognize students who excel in both academics and athletics.

In Onondaga County, New York, the public library started a program of basic reading instruction for deaf adults. In Broward County, Florida, a program provides a homelike setting for supervised visitation and parenting training for parents who are separated from their children due to abuse or domestic violence.

The needs for consumer protection, water quality, and affordable housing increase every year. Regional or local officials are elected to deal with issues such as public health, legal services, housing, and budget and fiscal management. They attend meetings and serve on committees. They know about the industry and agriculture of the area as well as the specific problems facing constituents, and they offer educated solutions, vote on laws, and generally represent the people in their districts.

There are two forms of county government: the commissioner/administrator form, in which the county board of commissioners appoints an *administrator* who serves the board, and the council/executive form, in which a *county executive* is the chief administrative officer of the district and has the power to veto ordinances enacted by the county board. A county government may include a *chief executive*, who directs regional services; *council members*, who are the *county legislators*; a *county clerk*, who keeps records of property titles, licenses, etc.; and a *county treasurer*, who is in charge of the receipt and disbursement of money.

County government funds come from sales tax, state aid, fees, and grants. A city government funds its projects and programs with money from sales and other local taxes, block grants, and state aid.

A city council president (*standing*) talks with council members during a break in a meeting. *(Daniel Mears, The Detroit News/AP Photo)*

Directing these funds and services are elected executives. *Mayors* serve as the heads of city governments and are elected by the general populace. Their specific functions vary depending on the structure of their government. In mayor-council governments, both the mayor and the city council are popularly elected. The council is responsible for formulating city ordinances, but the mayor exercises control over the actions of the council. In such governments, the mayor usually plays a dual role, serving not only as chief executive officer but also as an agent of the city government responsible for such functions as maintaining public order, security, and health. In a commission government, the people elect a number of *commissioners*, each of whom serves as head of a city department. The presiding commissioner is usually the mayor. The final type of municipal government is the council/manager form. Here, the council members are elected by the people, and one of their functions is to hire a *city manager* to administer the city departments. A mayor is elected by the council to chair the council and officiate at important municipal functions.

REQUIREMENTS

High School

Courses in government, civics, and history will give you an understanding of the structure of government. English courses are important because you will need good writing skills to communicate with constituents and other government officials. Math and accounting will help you develop analytical skills for examining statistics and demographics. Journalism classes will help you develop research and interview skills for identifying problems and developing programs.

Postsecondary Training

To serve on a local government, your experience and understanding of the city or county are generally more important than your educational background. Some mayors and council members are elected to their positions because they've lived in the region for a long time and have had experience with local industry and other concerns. For example, someone with years of farming experience may be the best candidate to serve a small agricultural community. Voters in local elections may be more impressed by a candidate's previous occupations and roles in the community than they are by a candidate's postsecondary degrees.

That said, most regional and local officials still hold an undergraduate degree, and many hold a graduate degree or a law degree.

Popular areas of study include public administration, law, economics, political science, history, and English. Regardless of your major as an undergraduate, you are likely to be required to take classes in English literature, statistics, foreign language, western civilization, and economics.

Other Requirements

To be successful in this field, you must deeply understand the city and region you serve. You need to be knowledgeable about the local industry, private businesses, and social problems. You should also have lived for some time in the region in which you hope to hold office.

You also need good people skills to be capable of listening to the concerns of constituents and other officials and exchanging ideas with them. Other useful qualities are problem-solving skills and creativity to develop innovative programs.

EXPLORING

Depending on the size of your city or county, you can probably become involved with your local government at a young age. Your council members and other government officials should be more accessible to you than state and federal officials, so take advantage of that. Visit the county court house and volunteer in whatever capacity you can with county-organized programs, such as tutoring in a literacy program or leading children's reading groups at the public library. Become involved with local elections.

Many candidates for local and state offices welcome young people to assist with campaigns. As a volunteer, you may make calls, post signs, and get to see a candidate at work. You will also have the opportunity to meet others who have an interest in government, and the experience will help you to gain a more prominent role in later campaigns.

Another way to learn about government is to become involved in an issue that interests you. Maybe there's an old building in your neighborhood you'd like to save from destruction, or maybe you have some ideas for youth programs or programs for senior citizens. Research what's being done about your concerns and come up with solutions to offer to local officials.

EMPLOYERS

Every city in the United States requires the services of local officials. In some cases, the services of a small town or suburb may be overseen by the government of a larger city or by the county government. According to the National Association of Counties, 48 states have operational county governments—a total of more than 3,060 counties. (Connecticut and Rhode Island are the only two states without counties.) The counties with the largest populations are Los Angeles County, California; Cook County, Illinois; and Harris County, Texas. There are also 33 governments that are consolidations of city and county governments; New York, Denver, and San Francisco are among them.

STARTING OUT

There is no direct career path for gaining public office. The way you pursue a local office will be greatly affected by the size and population of the region in which you live. When running for mayor or council of a small town, you may have no competition at all. On the other hand, to become mayor of a large city, you need extensive experience in the city's politics. If you're interested in pursuing a local position, research the backgrounds of your city mayor, county commissioners, and council members to get an idea of how they approached their political careers.

Some officials stumble into government offices after some success with political activism on the grassroots level. Others have had success in other areas, such as agriculture, business, and law enforcement, and use their particular understanding of an area to help improve the community. Many local politicians started their careers by assisting in someone else's campaign or advocating for an issue.

ADVANCEMENT

Some successful local and regional officials maintain their positions for many years. Others hold local office for only one or two terms, and then return full time to their businesses and other careers. Some local and regional officials choose to use a local position as a steppingstone to a position of greater power within the region or to a state office. Many mayors of the largest cities run for governor or state legislature and may eventually move into federal office.

EARNINGS

In general, salaries for government officials tend to be lower than what the official could make working in the private sector. In many local offices, officials volunteer their time or work only part time. City managers earned median annual salaries of $94,992 in 2008,

according to the U.S. Department of Labor (DOL). Chief administrators of cities and counties earned salaries that ranged from $50,000
to $261,166 in 2008–09, according to the International City/County
Management Association.

The DOL reports that government legislators earned median
annual salaries of $18,810 in 2009. Those in local government had
mean salaries of $36,780 in 2009. Salaries generally ranged from
less than $14,830 to more than $81,150, although some officials
earn nothing at all.

A job with a local or regional government may or may not provide
benefits. Some positions may include accounts for official travel and
other expenses.

WORK ENVIRONMENT

Most government officials work in a typical office setting. Some
may work a regular 40-hour week, while others work long hours
and weekends. Though some positions may only be considered part
time, they may take up nearly as many hours as full-time work.
Officials have the opportunity to meet with the people of the region,
but they also devote a lot of time to clerical duties. If serving a large
community, they may have assistants to help with phones, filing, and
preparing documents.

Because officials must be appointed or elected in order to keep
their jobs, determining long-range career plans can be difficult.
There may be extended periods of unemployment, where living off
of savings or other jobs may be necessary. Because of the low pay of
some positions, officials may have to work another job even while
they serve in office. This can result in little personal time and the
need to juggle many different responsibilities at once.

OUTLOOK

Though the form and structure of state and federal government are
not likely to change, the form of a local and county government can
be altered by popular vote. In every election, voters somewhere in
the country are deciding whether to keep their current forms of government or to introduce new forms. But these changes don't greatly
affect the number of officials needed to run a local government. The
chances of holding office will be greater in a smaller community. The
races for part-time and nonpaying offices will also be less competitive.

The issues facing a community will have the most effect on the
jobs of local officials. In a city with older neighborhoods, officials

deal with historic preservation, improvements in utilities, and water quality. In a growing city of many suburbs, officials have to make decisions regarding development, roads, and expanded routes for public transportation.

The federal government has made efforts to shift costs to the states. If this continues, states may offer less aid to counties. A county government's funds are also affected by changes in property taxes.

FOR MORE INFORMATION

For information on internships and to read Local Government Management: It's the Career For You!, *visit the ICMA Web site.*
International City/County Management Association (ICMA)
777 North Capitol Street, NE, Suite 500
Washington, DC 20002-4201
Tel: 202-289-4262
http://www.icma.org

For information on county governments, contact
National Association of Counties
25 Massachusetts Avenue, NW, Suite 500
Washington, DC 20001-1430
Tel: 202-393-6226
http://www.naco.org

For more information on finding a school, the master of public administration degree, and public affairs work, contact
**National Association of Schools of Public Affairs and
    Administration**
1029 Vermont Avenue, NW, Suite 1100
Washington, DC 20005-3517
Tel: 202-628-8965
E-mail: naspaa@naspaa.org
http://www.naspaa.org
http://www.gopublicservice.org

For information on cities, contact
National League of Cities
1301 Pennsylvania Avenue, NW, Suite 550
Washington, DC 20004-1747
Tel: 202-626-3000
E-mail: info@nlc.org
http://www.nlc.org

════════ INTERVIEW ════════

David Orr has been the Cook County (Illinois) clerk since 1990. He discussed his career in government with the editors of Careers in Focus: Politics.

Q. What are your primary and secondary responsibilities as Cook County clerk?

A. As Cook County clerk, I serve as the chief election authority for Cook County, one of the largest election jurisdictions in the nation. Along with administering elections in suburban Cook County, my office maintains birth, marriage, and death records; assists property owners in redeeming delinquent taxes; sets tax rates for 1,000-plus taxing bodies; and records the activity of the Cook County Board of Commissioners.

Q. How long have you worked as an elected official? What other jobs have you held in government?

A. Thirty-one years, having been elected alderman of the 49th Ward of Chicago in 1979. I served as former Mayor Harold Washington's vice mayor, and then as mayor after Washington's death in 1987.

Q. Why did you decide to pursue a career in government service?

A. I actually never made the decision to pursue a political career, per se. I thought the Chicago "machine" wasn't serving voters. I had been active in my neighborhood and decided to seek election so I could change that, but I never thought at the time it would become a career.

Q. What were your expectations entering politics/government? Are they much different from the realities?

A. I believe I was more realistic than most because I both taught and lived politics. I expected the "machine" to be brutal, corrupt, and yet powerful. Still, I was pleasantly surprised to see how supportive the voters were in bringing significant reforms to Chicago.

Q. How did you train for this job? What was your college major?

A. I majored in history in college, and I think liberal arts training is probably the best background you can get for politics. It is also useful to be a political activist and work with people on local and national issues. I gained experience in the field by serving as the campaign manager for a respected colleague who sought political office. And teaching college—particularly courses in government and the urban crisis—was invaluable.

Q. What are the most important personal and professional qualities for people in your career?

A. The most important personal quality is the desire to serve others, as opposed to wanting to make money for yourself. Professionally, it's important to be able to communicate well with people, to be able to juggle several tasks at one time, and to be sensitive to other people's backgrounds.

Q. What are some of the pros and cons of your job?

A. The pros: Among the biggest is the ability to make a difference in how democracy works and how government works to serve more people effectively. You also have the opportunity to set your own agenda, deal with important issues of the day, and the job forces you to learn constantly.

The cons: I believe very much in social and political change, and yet much of the politics in the Chicago area is dirty and corrupt. You have to work with some people by necessity, not by choice.

Q. What advice would you offer students as they graduate and look for jobs in government?

A. As it may take awhile to get what you want, it's sometimes important to volunteer for activities—be they political or cultural—to become known in your community. Understand that there are various ways to aggressively pursue a job, including being willing to better prepare yourself and listening carefully to learn if your skills fall short. Perhaps the most important, though, is to find someone who will give you a straight answer so you avoid waiting years for things that will never materialize.

Q. What are some of the rewards and challenges of running for office?

A. The biggest reward is educating the electorate and learning from them at the same time. It is a challenge learning how to deal with hostile people, and merging your goals and positions with the voters' needs and frustrations. Finally, it's essential to both know the issues and how to get things done.

Q. **What do you consider your greatest achievement as Cook County clerk?**

A. I'm proud of our victories that dramatically improved voter registration and access to voting—motor voter, early voting, teen judges, and error detection. These programs and enhancements revolutionized the way we register voters, provide greater opportunity for people to cast ballots, engage students in the political process, and give voters a second chance to correct mistakes on their ballots.

Q. **Where would you like to be professionally in five or 10 years?**

A. I'd like to have the opportunity to work for significant social and political change. I'd hope to be respected as a knowledgeable, straight-talking politician who cares for and understands the voters' needs.

Urban and Regional Planners

OVERVIEW

Urban and regional planners assist in the development and redevelopment of a city, metropolitan area, or region. They work to preserve historical buildings, protect the environment, and help manage a community's growth and change. Planners evaluate individual buildings and city blocks, and are also involved in the design of new subdivisions, neighborhoods, and even entire towns. A majority of planners work at the local level; when employed in this setting they are also known as *community* or *city planners*. There are approximately 38,400 urban and regional planners working in the United States.

HISTORY

Cities have always been planned to some degree. Most cultures, from the ancient Greeks to the Chinese to the Native Americans, made some organized plans for the development of their cities. By the fourth century B.C., theories of urban planning existed in the writings of Plato, Aristotle, and Hippocrates. Their ideas concerning the issues of site selection and orientation were later modified and updated by Vitruvius in his *De architectura*, which appeared after 27 B.C. This work helped create a standardized guide for Roman engineers as they built fortified settlements and cities throughout the vast empire. Largely inspired by Vitruvius, 15th-century Italian theorists compiled enormous amounts of information and ideas on urban planning. They replaced

> ## Facts About Urban and Regional Planners, 2010
>
> - The typical urban planner was 43 years old and had worked in the field for 14 years.
> - The most popular practice specialty for planners was community development and redevelopment.
> - Planners earned the highest median salaries in the following states (in descending order): District of Columbia, California, Nevada, and New Jersey.
>
> Source: American Planning Association/American Institute of Certified Planners 2010 *Planners Salary Survey*

vertical walls with angular fortifications for better protection during times of war. They also widened streets and opened up squares by building new churches, halls, and palaces. Early designs were based on a symmetrical style that quickly became fashionable in many of the more prosperous European cities.

Modern urban planning owes much to the driving force of the industrial revolution. The desire for more sanitary living conditions led to the demolition of slums. Laws were enacted to govern new construction and monitor the condition of old buildings. In 1848, Baron George Eugene Haussmann organized the destruction and replacement of 40 percent of the residential quarters in Paris and created new neighborhood park systems. In England, the Public Health Act of 1875 allowed municipalities to regulate new construction, the removal of waste, and newly constructed water and sewer systems.

Today, as the U.S. population continues to grow, urban and regional planners are playing an increasingly important role in developing and redeveloping communities of all sizes.

THE JOB

Urban and regional planners assist in the development or maintenance of carefully designed communities. Working for a government agency or as a consultant, planners are involved in integrating new buildings, houses, sites, and subdivisions into an overall city plan. Their plans must coordinate streets, traffic, public facilities, water and sewage, transportation, safety, and ecological factors such as wildlife habitats, wetlands, and floodplains. Planners are also involved in renovating and preserving historic buildings. They work with a variety of professionals, including architects, artists, computer programmers, engineers, economists, landscape architects, land developers, lawyers, writers, and environmental and other special interest groups.

Chris Wayne works as a redevelopment planner for the city of Omaha, Nebraska. His work involves identifying new project sites—buildings that the planning department wants to redevelop and going about acquiring the property. Before making a purchase, he hires an appraiser to determine the worth of the building and then makes an offer to the building's owner. If the owner accepts and the building is slated for redevelopment, the city may have to vacate the building. "This involves interviewing the residents," Wayne says, "to determine what's necessary for them to move. We determine what amount they'll be compensated." Various community programs assist in finding new housing or providing tenants with moving funds. Once the property has been vacated, the planning department accepts and reviews proposals from developers. A developer is then offered a contract. When demolition and construction begin, Wayne's department must monitor the project and make the necessary payments.

Urban and regional planners also work with unused or undeveloped land. They may help design the layout for a proposed building, keeping in mind traffic circulation, parking, and the use of open space. Planners are also responsible for suggesting ways to implement these programs or proposals, considering their costs and how to raise funds for them.

Schools, churches, recreational areas, and residential tracts are studied to determine how they will fit into designs for optimal usefulness and beauty. As with other factors, specifications for the nature and kinds of buildings must be considered. Zoning codes, which regulate the specific use of land and buildings, must be adhered to during construction. Planners need to be knowledgeable of these regulations and other legal matters and communicate them to builders and developers.

Some urban and regional planners teach in colleges and schools of planning, and many do consulting work. Planners today are concerned not only with city codes, but also with environmental problems of water pollution, solid waste disposal, water treatment plants, and public housing.

Planners work in older cities or design new ones. Columbia, Maryland, and Reston, Virginia, both built in the 1960s, are examples of planned communities. Before plans for such communities can be developed, planners must prepare detailed maps and charts showing the proposed use of land for housing, business, and community needs. These studies provide information on the types of industries in the area, the locations of housing developments and businesses, and the plans for providing basic needs such as water, sewage treatment, and transportation. After maps and charts have been analyzed, planners design the layout to present to land developers, city officials, housing experts, architects, and construction firms. Many planners use geographic information systems (GIS) software to design these layouts. GIS software allows planners to create electronic maps of land areas. They can then overlay these maps with geographic variables such as topographical data or population density. This technology allows them to work faster and create alternative plans for land development.

The following short descriptions list the wide variety of planners within the field.

Human services planners develop health and social service programs to upgrade living standards for those lacking opportunities or resources. These planners frequently work for private health care organizations and government agencies.

Historic preservation planners use their knowledge of the law and economics to help preserve historic buildings, sites, and neighborhoods. They are frequently employed by state agencies, local governments, and the National Park Service.

Transportation planners, working mainly for government agencies, oversee the transportation infrastructure of a community, keeping in mind local priorities such as economic development and environmental concerns.

Housing, social, and community development planners analyze housing needs to identify potential opportunities and problems that may affect a neighborhood and its surrounding communities. Such planners are usually employed by private real estate and financial firms, local governments, and community development organizations.

Economic development planners, usually employed by local governments or chambers of commerce, focus on attracting and retaining industry to a specific community. They communicate with industry leaders who select sites for new plants, warehouses, and other major projects.

Environmental planners advocate the integration of environmental issues into building construction, land use, and other community objectives. They work at all levels of government and for some nonprofit organizations.

Urban design planners work to design and locate public facilities, such as churches, libraries, and parks, to best serve the larger community. Employers include large-scale developers, private consulting firms, and local governments.

International development planners specialize in strategies for transportation, rural development, modernization, and urbanization. They are frequently employed by international agencies, such as the United Nations, and by national governments in less developed countries.

REQUIREMENTS

High School

You should take courses in government and social studies to learn about the past and present organizational structure of cities and counties. You need good communication skills for working with people in a variety of professions, so take courses in speech and English composition. Drafting, architecture, and art classes will familiarize you with the basics of design. Become active on your student council so that you can be involved in implementing changes for the school community.

Postsecondary Training

A bachelor's degree is the minimum requirement for most trainee jobs with federal, state, or local government boards and agencies. However, more opportunities for employment and advancement are available to those with a master's degree in urban or regional planning or a related field, such as environmental planning, urban design, or geography. For those who major in urban and regional planning, specializations are often available in community development and redevelopment, environmental and natural resources planning, land-use or code enforcement, transportation planning, urban design, and economic planning and development. Typical courses include geography, public administration, political science, law, engineering, architecture, landscape architecture, real estate, finance, and management. Computer courses and training in statistical techniques and geographic information systems are also essential. Most master's programs last a minimum of two years and require students to participate in internships with city planning departments.

When considering schools, check with the American Planning Association (http://www.planning.org) for a list of accredited undergraduate and graduate planning programs. The association can also direct you to scholarship and fellowship programs available to students enrolled in planning programs.

Certification or Licensing

Although not a requirement, obtaining certification in urban and regional planning can lead to more challenging, better-paying positions. The American Institute of Certified Planners, a division of the American Planning Association (APA), grants certification to planners who meet certain academic and professional requirements and successfully complete an examination. The exam tests for knowledge of the history and future of planning, research methods, plan implementation, and other relevant topics.

The state of New Jersey requires planners to be licensed. The state of Michigan requires those who want to practice under the title of "community planner" to be licensed. Contact these states' departments of labor for more information on licensing requirements.

Other Requirements

Chris Wayne pursued a master's degree in urban studies because he was drawn to community development. "I was interested in the social interaction of people and the space they occupy, such as parks and plazas," he says.

In addition to being interested in planning, you should have design skills and a good understanding of spatial relationships. Good analytical skills will help you in evaluating projects. Planners must be able to visualize the relationships between streets, buildings, parks, and other developed spaces and anticipate potential planning problems. As a result, logic and problem-solving abilities are also important.

EXPLORING

Research the origins of your city by visiting your county courthouse and local library. Check out early photographs and maps of your area to give you an idea of what went into the planning of your community. Visit local historic areas to learn about the development and history behind old buildings. You may also consider getting involved in efforts to preserve local buildings and areas that are threatened.

With the help of a teacher or academic adviser, arrange an interview with a working planner to gain details of his or her job. Another good way to see what planners do is to attend a meeting of a local planning commission, which by law is open to the public. Interested students can find out details about upcoming meetings through their local paper or planning office.

EMPLOYERS

There are approximately 38,400 urban and regional planners working in the United States. Sixty-six percent of planners work for local governments; others work for state agencies, the federal government, and in the private sector (for companies involved with management, scientific, and technical consulting services and architectural and engineering companies).

Many planners are hired for full-time work where they intern. Others choose to seek other opportunities, such as with state and federal governments and nonprofit organizations. Planners work for government agencies that focus on particular areas of city research and development, such as transportation, the environment, and housing. Urban and regional planners are also sought by colleges, law firms, the United Nations, and even foreign governments of rapidly modernizing countries.

STARTING OUT

With a bachelor's degree, a beginning worker may start out as an assistant at an architectural firm or construction office. Others start out working as city planning aides in regional or urban offices. New planners research projects, conduct interviews, survey the field, and write reports on their findings. Those with a master's degree can enter the profession at a higher level, working for federal, state, and local agencies.

Previous work experience in a planning office or with an architectural or engineering firm is useful before applying for a job with city, county, or regional planning agencies. Membership in a professional organization is also helpful in locating job opportunities. These include the American Planning Association, the American Institute of Architects, the American Society of Civil Engineers, and the International City/County Management Association. Most of these organizations host student chapters that provide information on internship opportunities and professional publications. (See the end of this article for contact information.)

Because many planning staffs are small, directors are usually eager to fill positions quickly. As a result, job availability can be highly variable. Students are advised to apply for jobs before they complete their degree requirements. Most colleges have career services offices to assist students in finding job leads.

ADVANCEMENT

Beginning assistants can advance within the planning board or department to eventually become planners. The positions of senior planner and planning director are successive steps in some agencies. Frequently, experienced planners obtain advancement by moving to a larger city or county planning board, where they become responsible for larger and more complicated projects, make policy decisions, or become responsible for funding new developments. Other planners may become consultants to communities that cannot afford a full-time planner. Some planners also serve as city managers, cabinet secretaries, and presidents of consulting firms.

EARNINGS

Earnings vary based on position, work experience, and the population of the city or town the planner serves. According to the U.S. Department of Labor (DOL), median annual earnings of urban and regional planners were $61,820 in 2009. The lowest paid 10 percent earned less than $39,460, and the highest paid 10 percent earned $94,800 or more. Mean annual earnings in local government, the industry employing the largest numbers of urban and regional planners, were $62,170. Those employed by the federal government had mean annual earnings of $88,230. Certified planners earn $13,000 more a year than planners who are not certified, according to the American Planning Association.

Because many planners work for government agencies, they usually have sick leave and vacation privileges and are covered by retirement and health plans. Many planners also have access to a city automobile.

Planners who work as consultants are generally paid on a fee basis. Their earnings are often high and vary greatly according to their reputations and work experience. Their earnings will depend on the number of consulting jobs they accept. They typically do not receive fringe benefits.

WORK ENVIRONMENT

Planners spend a considerable amount of time in an office setting. However, in order to gather data about the areas they develop, planners also spend much of their time outdoors examining the surrounding land, structures, and traffic. Most planners work standard 40-hour weeks, but they may also attend evening or weekend council meetings or public forums to share upcoming development proposals.

Planners work alone and with land developers, public officials, civic leaders, and citizens' groups. Occasionally, they may face opposition from interest groups against certain development proposals and, as a result, they must have the patience needed to work with disparate groups. The job can be stressful when trying to keep tight deadlines or when defending proposals in both the public and private sectors.

OUTLOOK

The DOL expects the overall demand for urban and regional planners to grow faster than the average for all careers through 2018. Communities turn to professional planners for help in meeting demands resulting from urbanization and the growth in population. Urban and regional planners are needed to zone and plan land use for undeveloped and rural areas as well as commercial development in rapidly growing suburban areas. There will be jobs available with nongovernmental agencies that deal with historic preservation and redevelopment. Opportunities also exist in maintaining existing bridges, highways, and sewers, and in preserving and restoring historic sites and buildings. Opportunities should be best in wealthy communities that are experiencing rapid growth. These communities need planners to help them plan for new roads, sewer systems, schools, and other facilities within the budget set by the town.

The DOL predicts that job growth will be fastest in the private sector—mainly at companies that provide professional, scientific, and technical services.

Factors that may affect job growth include government regulation regarding the environment, housing, transportation, and land use. The continuing redevelopment of inner-city areas and the expansion of suburban areas will serve to provide many jobs for planners. However, when communities face budgetary constraints, planning departments may be reduced before others, such as police departments or education.

Planners with graduate degrees in urban and regional planning or related fields and knowledge of geographic information system technology will have the best employment prospects.

FOR MORE INFORMATION

For more information on architectural careers, contact
American Institute of Architects
1735 New York Avenue, NW
Washington, DC 20006-5292
Tel: 800-242-3837
E-mail: infocentral@aia.org
http://www.aia.org

For more information on careers, certification, and accredited planning programs, contact
American Planning Association
205 North Michigan Avenue, Suite 1200
Chicago, IL 60601-3009
Tel: 312-431-9100
E-mail: customerservice@planning.org
http://www.planning.org

For information in civil engineering, contact
American Society of Civil Engineers
1801 Alexander Bell Drive
Reston, VA 20191-5467
Tel: 800-548-2723
http://www.asce.org

For information on planning careers and undergraduate and graduate training in planning, contact
Association of Collegiate Schools of Planning
6311 Mallard Trace
Tallahassee, FL 32312-1570
Tel: 850-385-2054
http://www.acsp.org

To learn about city management and the issues affecting today's cities, visit this Web site or contact
International City/County Management Association
777 North Capitol Street, NE, Suite 500
Washington, DC 20002-4201
Tel: 202-289-4262
http://www.icma.org

Index

Entries and page numbers in **bold** indicate major treatment of a topic.